"*I'm a fatalist. I try to live and enjoy every moment as it exists. Think about tomorrow but don't worry about it. I really enjoy life. I relish it. I enjoy now! If I had to write my own epitaph it would be: 'Here lies Elizabeth Taylor. Thank you for every moment, good and bad. I've enjoyed it all!'* "

ELIZABETH TAYLOR: TRIUMPHS and TRAGEDIES—the story of a woman who has become a legend in her own time.

Elizabeth Taylor

TRIUMPHS & TRAGEDIES

BILL ADLER

ace books

A Division of Charter Communications Inc.
A GROSSET & DUNLAP COMPANY
51 Madison Avenue
New York, New York 10010

An ACE Original

First Ace Printing: February 1982
Published simultaneously in Canada

2 4 6 8 0 9 7 5 3 1
Manufactured in the United States of America

CHAPTER ONE
Roots

The cat is the only animal gifted with nine lives. Most mortals have but one. The exceptions are usually notable. It is interesting to note that in one of her varied nine lives, Elizabeth Taylor played the part of a "cat"—Maggie, the cat on the hot tin roof.

Her first life was auspicious from the beginning; she became the moppet movie star at the age of nine—Little Miss Elizabeth Taylor.

Her second life transformed her for a time into a loving wife—Mrs. Conrad Nicholas Hilton.

Her third life changed her into a wife and mother of two—Mrs. Michael Wilding.

Her fourth life culminated in death and tragedy and created a grieving widow—Mrs. Mike Todd.

Her fifth life made her into a home-wrecker—Mrs. Eddie Fisher.

Her sixth life brought her millions of dollars and worldwide fame—Cleopatra, 1960's-style.

Her seventh life made her a household word—Mrs. Richard Jenkins Burton.

Her eighth life led her down the trail of politics
—Mrs. Senator John Warner.

Her ninth life returned her to the public eye on
the most exalted podium in the country, the Broadway stage as—Broadway Superstar.

If nine is the magic number, perhaps that is the
last of Elizabeth Rosemond Taylor Hilton Wilding
Todd Fisher Burton Warner's many trans-
mogrifications.

But don't be too sure.

This so obviously American story of success and
wealth and power began, ironically enough, not in
the United States, but in England.

In fact, when the motion picture *National Velvet*
catapulted its young heroine into international
fame at the tender age of twelve, most moviegoers
firmly believed that Eliabeth Taylor was an English
actress. She spoke with a pure British accent. She
looked English.

True, she was born in England, but she was as
American as, well, Elizabeth Taylor twenty years
later! Her parents were Americans too, from heart-
land U.S.A.—Illinois and Kansas.

She was born on February 27, 1932, in a Geor-
gian house in the nouveau-riche section of
Hampstead, London, where her parents were living
at the time. The records, registered in the district of
Hendon, show that she weighed eight and a half
pounds at birth.

Beautiful? By no means, according to an unim-
peachable source: her mother. "She was the *fun-
niest*-looking baby I have ever seen!" She was covered with the basic black hair that was to become
one of her most recognizable features through the

years; her ears had thick black fuzz, the sides of her head were covered with hair; *too much* hair!

And those eyes—those eyes sometimes described as sapphire blue, sometimes described as violet, sometimes described as purple, sometimes described as blue—*they* weren't even open. In fact, they kept shut for ten days after her birth. When they did open, they were that deep exceptional blue, framed by a set of double basic black lashes.

Soon, of course, people would find themselves staring in fascination at the eyes of Elizabeth Taylor and gasp: "*Look* at those eyes!"

Because she had American parents and because she was indeed born in England, she was technically a citizen of both England and of America. And so people who saw her in pictures when she was twelve and thought she was English were right; but even by that time she was unmistakably American.

Her mother was born in Arkansas City, Kansas, near the Oklahoma border, and grew up there as Sara Warmbrodt. Sara was a remarkably good-looking girl. She had an easy way with her and a charming manner. Her father was of German stock and worked as an engineer in the Empire Laundry. Her mother, Anna, was a musician.

Sara wanted to train at Georgia Brown's dramatic school in Kansas City, but her mother put her foot down. "Never will we have an actress in this family." But after some more argument, the family gave in and Sara enrolled at the school.

She changed her name from Warmbrodt to Sothern and as Sara Sothern worked in stock companies in Sioux City; Haverhill, Mass.; Winnipeg;

and Los Angeles. In L.A. she was hired by the Edward Everett Horton Repertory Group, a stock company operating out of the Majestic Theater. She got her big part there, playing the crippled girl cured by a faith healer in a Channing Pollack tear-jerker titled *The Fool*.

The play had long runs in Los Angeles, New York, and London. London gave Sara an ovation —the reserved British audience breaking down and calling out, "Bravo, bravo, bravo!"

From *The Fool* Sara Sothern went to Broadway to play in *The Little Spitfire*. But something had happened in London that changed her life. She had met a man there whom she had known years before at Arkansas City High School. His name was Francis Taylor.

The Taylors had their roots in mid-America, too. Francis Taylor had grown up in Arkansas City, entering Arkansas City High in 1912, a year after Sara started. He was quite simply one of the handsomest teenagers at the school. He was tall, with dark black hair—hair like his daughter's famous hair—and he had the family trade mark: blue eyes with thick dark double-lined lashes. There was an Irish look to him; but, curiously enough, he was strictly of Scottish and English origin. He had excellent taste in clothes; he always looked right.

The word was that Francis's mother, also called Elizabeth Rosemond Taylor, was a great beauty of her day, chiefly known for the thick black hair that made her granddaughter world famous. Francis's father, Francis Senior, was a successful businessman who had left Indiana in 1890 to make his fortune in Arkansas City.

Shortly after Sara dropped out of Arkansas City High, Francis left, too. At the age of sixteen he went to work for his uncle in St. Louis. His uncle was Howard Young, a hardnosed businessman who had made a fortune in family portraits.

Young's wife was Mabel Rosemond, Elizabeth Rosemond's sister. Mabel Rosemond was as much a classic beauty as Elizabeth Rosemond. The two women nurtured a natural rivalry that lasted throughout their lives.

Young left his home in Belle Center, Ohio, when he was ten years old, in 1882, and began to collect family photographs and transform them into "portraits." He did it by a simple chemical process that changed the tintypes into beautiful portraits. These he mounted in oval frames and sold. He prospered. At eighteen, he was worth $400,000.

The Depression of 1896 wiped him out and he started in again. Times had changed. His clients were more sophisticated. Now he had family photographs copied in oil on canvas by artists and then framed. One of his prospects asked him to locate some nice works of art and buy them for him. Young did so, discovering that he had a natural flair as an art dealer.

Soon the rich industrialist Fisher family and Ford family of Detroit became his clients. He moved to New York and his nephew Francis joined him. Meanwhile, Mabel, his wife, became an alcoholic. Tension was increased between the two sides of the family.

Working for his hard-driving uncle was not all fun and games for Francis Taylor. Young was a rough taskmaster and an unforgiving boss. He was also tight-fisted, a "wealthy man who was not inclined to share it," as one reference had it.

But Francis finally learned the trade and his uncle sent him to Europe to scout out art works. His job was to travel and buy old masters and modern works to sell in New York.

He opened a gallery in London at 30 Old Bond Street, using it as his headquarters. It was there he happened to see Sara in her play in the East End and took her out. When he returned on a visit to his uncle in New York, Sara was playing in *The Little Spitfire*. He took her out again.

They were both young and handsome and likable, and they struck it off well together. They were married in 1926. Sara Sothern gave up the stage as easily as she had given up life in Arkansas City, and the two of them traveled over Europe together—Berlin, Florence, Ireland, Milan, Paris, Rome, Scotland, Switzerland, Vienna.

"Everywhere we found paintings," Sara later said.

Meanwhile the Taylors made a connection in London that was to serve them for the rest of their lives. Victor Cazalet was a bachelor, and a Conservative Member of Parliament. Dashing, wealthy, gregarious, and handsome, he was everything the English aristocracy stood for. He and his sister, Mrs. Thelma Cazalet-Keir, and his mother, Mollie (Maud) Cazalet, were inseparable.

Cazalet was a typical British sportsman, was well brought up, and loved to collect art. It was through art that he found the Taylors. This common interest was coupled with another more powerful one: the Taylors and the Cazalets were ardent Christian Scientists.

One of Cazalet's favorite artists was a typically bohemian painter named Augustus John; John became a passion for Taylor, too. Cazalet, his sister Thelma, and his mother "took up" the Taylors and introduced them into the world of aristocracy, royalty, and the literati.

After three years of travel, Sara Taylor found herself pregnant. With the Cazalets' help, the Taylors found a neo-Georgian house in London on Wildwood Road, facing out over Hampstead Heath. English houses like that always had names, and this was no exception. The Taylors settled into "Heathwood."

Their first child, a boy named Howard, was born in 1929. And it was to Heathwood that Elizabeth Rosemond Taylor came in early 1932. She was named Elizabeth after Sara's mother—and after Francis's mother as well. In Sara Taylor's memoirs, she said her daughter was named Rosemond after "her Aunt Mabel Rosemond Young." It was always good to mention the Young connection as much as possible. Elizabeth Rosemond Taylor's maternal grandmother, of course, was actually the *original* Elizabeth Rosemond Taylor. So much for origins.

Heathwood was a fine city home, but the Taylors needed a country place as well. And once again Cazalet helped out. The Cazalet estate was located in Kent, in an idyllic country setting. The main house was called "Great Swifts." But like all English estates, there were numerous cottages scattered about. One of these was named "Little Swallows"—to put it into perspective with "Great Swifts." And it was here that Cazalet invited the Taylors to spend their summers. The Taylors didn't even pay to rent the house. It was theirs free.

According to the legend, Little Swallows was a sixteenth century house that had figured in Jeffery Farnol's novel *The Broad Highway*. In the novel Farnol called it the "Haunted House." But it wasn't haunted. It was a beautiful place. And it was here that the young Taylor children learned to live the fabulous English country life—full of fields and animals and the sporting life. They learned to ride horseback, as well, a skill that would be most important for Elizabeth later.

From the time she was very small, Elizabeth formed attachments to all kinds of animals. She named every one of them, usually after people she knew. One day her mother found her talking to someone in the garden named "Elmer." When she asked her daughter who Elmer was, Elizabeth handed her mother a fat squishy fishing worm. That was Sara's last time to ask *that* question.

There were dogs and cats as well, with whom Elizabeth conversed. But the most important animal at Little Swallows was a pony named Betty. Betty had been presented to Elizabeth as a special gift from her "godfather"—Victor Cazalet—and her "godmother"—Mollie Cazalet.

What happened when Elizabeth first met her pony is interesting from a standpoint of Elizabeth's later character and personality. At the time she saw the pony, no one knew how unpredictable the mare really was. It was originally a wild New Forest pony that was caught and trained as a milk horse. It was so old that it was considered very safe for children to ride.

Howard, who had three years on his sister, decided to show her how to handle a horse. He hopped onto Betty and rode her around the garden. The idea was to show Elizabeth how to sit the horse, how to hold the reins. Betty performed superbly for Howard.

Finally Elizabeth reached out her arms. She wanted to ride in back of her brother. Her father lifted her up and she held on to Howard's waist. And that was not what Betty wanted. She reverted to unpredictability, stomped, and bucked the two children off her back.

Elizabeth crashed into a patch of stinging nettles. She had to be rubbed down with dock weed until the swelling and burning subsided. But that wasn't the end of the episode. She took a long look at Betty, and then walked over to her, leading her around the garden and quietly talking to her the way a cowboy talks to a horse to gentle it.

Finally she took the mare over to a stone wall and climbed up on its back. She lay stomachdown on Betty's back, held her around the neck, and kept on talking. The mare sauntered off into the fields, and never again bucked her off.

It was when she was three that Elizabeth had her first long and serious illness—an illness that was a precursor to many more that would affect her through the years. What started out as a simple sore throat wound up with abscessed ears that had to be lanced over and over again. Her illness went on for weeks and weeks. Hot poultices were applied to both ears day and night. Her ears had to be probed and dressed continually. For three weeks her temperature hovered near 103 degrees.

Finally the fever broke and she recovered. Illness

would strike her again and again with the same results: long and enduring pain, serious complications, and finally relief and cure.

Elizabeth took ballet lessons, the same way any
other self-respecting young lady of the time did,
but her lessons were taught by Madame Vacani,
the ballet mistress to the Royal Family. "Madame
Vacani" was really simply Mrs. Rankin, but she
was one-quarter Italian. Howard had been learning
the steps, but everyone thought Elizabeth was too
young to dance. But she wasn't. She appeared in a
recital in Queen's Hall, for the benefit of a hospital.
Elizabeth, Duchess of York, and her daughters, the
Princesses Elizabeth and Margaret Rose, attended.

Elizabeth was one of dozens of angels, fairies
and butterflies. At the finale, the girls all went
down in deep curtsies, arms extended back of them
like wings, hands fluttering. Curtain. Curtain call.
Everybody off.

All but one. There lay Elizabeth, face to the
floor, fluttering—*alone* in the middle of the stage.
Suddenly realizing she was alone, she leaped to her
feet to flutter off. But there was applause. She
circled around and around and curtsied again.

And of course it was there that she caught the
fever to act—so her mother said. "Elizabeth had
inherited a certain amount of 'ham,'" she wrote.

For her first seven years, Elizabeth lived in that
idyllic setting of Heathwood and Little Swallows.
Gradually she grew out of her toddler stage and
became a young girl. But it was her brother who
was always called the *beautiful* child. With long
golden hair, blue eyes, and regular features, he was
almost what Sara called him: a "Botticelli angel."

She had been warned by her mother when she was carrying him that she should keep her mind full of beautiful thoughts to have a beautiful baby. And it worked with Howard.

"What," Sara wondered, "had happened to my beautiful thoughts before my daughter was born?"

It was most annoying to her to have to listen to people who looked at Howard and then at Elizabeth, and compared the flowing golden locks and the basic black hair, and turned to her and commiserated: "Poor little girl. Isn't it too bad she isn't the boy, and Howard the girl?"

Customers in the Taylor gallery on Old Bond Street would frequently see the children there, left by Sara on a shopping tour. One assistant said: "People who came into the gallery would remark of the beauty of the children. But most that saw the two of them would praise the boy."

Apparently Elizabeth made note of that.

On the Continent Adolf Hitler was engaged in diplomatic bullying, but in 1939 it turned real and he annexed what remained of Czechoslovakia.

About that time Victor Cazalet had a private interview with the future Prime Minister, Winston Churchill. Within hours he was at Little Swallows closeted with Taylor. There was going to be trouble. The Taylors decided that their children were not to be involved in it. Two weeks later Sara and Howard and Elizabeth were on their way to New York on the S.S. *Manhattan*.

Elizabeth's grandfather, Sara's father, was living out on the West Coast at the time, where he had gone in the late Twenties to start a chicken ranch. The Taylors settled in Pasadena, where Sara enrolled Howard and Elizabeth in Willard School. The superintendent introduced them at an assembly to the student body, pointing out that they had been brought up in England and would therefore talk "differently."

Within months they were beginning to lose their accents, although they continued to speak correctly without any prompting. But it wasn't Elizabeth's pronunciation that fascinated everyone who met her. It was the eyes and hair. Besides that, she bore an uncanny resemblance to Vivian Leigh, who had just been cast as Scarlett O'Hara in David Selznick's motion picture *Gone With the Wind*. There was a search on for someone to play Bonnie, her daughter in the picture.

"That child is the image of Vivien Leigh!" people would say. "Has the little girl ever been in pictures?" When Sara said no, she added that she wouldn't want her to be.

"We didn't want her in pictures. We just wanted her to have a normal life."

At least, that was Sara's version.

Sam Marx, about whom more later, hooted at reading Sara's statement. "Her parents moved heaven and earth to get their child into pictures," he said. Elizabeth Taylor's first agent, Jules Goldstone, corroborated that, with one slight alteration: "Never talk about Liz's *parents,* talk about *Sara.*"

But in those first few months in California there were no movie deals.

In December Francis Taylor brought in crates and crates of paintings from the London gallery, including a large collection of paintings and drawings by Augustus John. He opened a gallery in the

Château Elysée in Hollywood, using a suite of rooms leased from the management. Because it was too far to commute to the gallery from Pasadena, the family decided to move in closer to Hollywood. The Taylors found a house in Pacific Palisades.

"I wanted to be an actress," Elizabeth wrote later in her memoirs. "One day the teacher had each child stand up and tell what he wanted to be and why. . . . I said *I* wanted to be an actress." When everybody laughed at her, Elizabeth did a slow burn. These were the sons and daughters of real actresses and producers—Katy and Irving Shearer, Darrylin and Susan Zanuck—and she realized she had made a mistake. She did exactly what you would think Elizabeth Taylor would do. She struck a haughty pose, and delivered the punch line: "I don't want to be a *movie star,*" she said, "I want to be a serious actress like my mother was."

Oddly enough, Elizabeth's first crush was on one of her school mates at Pacific Palisades. As they were hurrying down the hall in a crowd, he accidentally tripped her, and then leaned down to pick her up. "Hi, there, beautiful!" he said. She went limp with ecstasy. His name was "something like Derek Hansen," Elizabeth recalled. "Later he changed it to John Derek."

The creator of Bo Derek did not reciprocate her affection, but ignored her. When other boys began to express interest in her, Elizabeth rejected them. "I always kicked them and belted them," she recalled. "One poor little boy tried to kiss me and, oh, God, did I beat him up." She could not remember his name.

It was not Darryl Zanuck, or Norma Shearer, or

Derek Hansen/John Derek who was instrumental in introducing Elizabeth to the motion picture business, but rather the temperamental tosspot artist and longhair bohemian named Augustus John.

Andrea Berens, soon to become Andrea Cowdin, the wife of J. Cheever Cowdin, the chairman of Universal Studios, had been painted once by Augustus John in England. She was a great admirer of his work. Scouting out some of his paintings at Taylor's gallery with Reggie Allen, head of the story department of Universal, the two of them had lunch with the Taylors and Elizabeth one Saturday.

Always on the lookout for good movie talent, Andrea drew Sara aside. "I would like Cheever to see Elizabeth."

Sara invited Cowdin and Andrea to tea the following day.

The upshot of the whole thing was that Cowdin fell under Elizabeth's spell as much as his wife-to-be. He insisted that Sara bring her daughter to the studio for a screen test. "She's a natural for pictures," Cowdin said.

CHAPTER TWO
Three Inches to Stardom

The world of celluloid was a world quite different from the real one outside. It was a world to which sound had been added to sight. Sound meant song, so, everyone who played in films sang. Even Clark Gable and Cary Grant sang in some of their early movies.

All little girls in this strange shadowy world sang. Shirley Temple burst into song every ten minutes on cue. So did Deanna Durbin. So did Judy Garland. Elizabeth Taylor knew that to make good in the movies she must sing. But, frankly, she wasn't very good.

Sara once sat down at the piano, not even knowing how to play, and began hitting notes. Elizabeth tried to sing the notes, and sometimes succeeded. "I couldn't hit a note for the life of me, at first," she said later. "But finally I got so I could sing a little song."

By the time she had been invited to appear at Universal, she could almost carry a tune. The ex-

citement of the challenge charged her up. Savoring
the promise of a trip to Universal, Elizabeth and
her mother proceeded to her dancing class the
following Monday at Mr. Sheehee's on La
Cienaga.

The class was filled with offspring of the rich and
powerful in Hollywood: Judy and Barbara Goetz,
the granddaughters of Louis B. Mayer; the Zanuck
children; and Erin Considine, the daughter of John
Considine, a producer at Metro-Goldwyn-Mayer.

Elizabeth was so full of herself that she joined in
with another girl who was sitting at the piano
playing and singing—and warbled with her untrained voice along with the other girl. In fact, she
was actually imitating some of the animals she so
loved—her singing had a weird birdlike quality.

Erin Considine's mother, Carmen, drew Sara
aside and suggested that she let her husband at
M.G.M. see and hear Elizabeth. That was almost
too much for Sara; she told her that Elizabeth was
scheduled for a screen test at Universal. Carmen
made her promise not to sign anything until her
husband had seen Elizabeth.

Because the Universal appointment had been set
for later in the week, Sara took Elizabeth first to
Considine in Culver City. Considine took one look
at her, listened to her, and sent her to Louis B.
Mayer. Mayer was sitting in his enormous office
with a dozen of the top brass. Elizabeth was introduced around.

She talked to each one of them. Elizabeth had a
photographic memory, and she remembered all the
names. When Mayer finally asked her to sing, she
made up a song on the spur of the moment, about
the men in the room. She named every one of them,

using their names.

The big pay-off came when she sang in her very off-key voice: "I love you, Mr. Mayer; you are simply marvelous, Mr. Mannix." That did it. It was pure Hollywood hokum; it was so bad it was good. She didn't *need* a screen test. "With training," Mayer said, "she may become a great singer. We want her."

Sara hesitated, because she had promised Universal she would bring in Elizabeth. She kept her word and did not sign. The following day Elizabeth and her mother went over to Universal but found that Cowdin was in New York. He was reached by telephone, told that Elizabeth had been offered a contract by M.G.M. Cowdin did not hesitate.

"If M.G.M. wants her, I want her. I'll double their offer." M.G.M.'s offer was the standard $100 a week. "Two hundred a week!"

Meanwhile, Dan Kelley, Universal's casting director, took a long hard look at Elizabeth. He didn't particularly like what he saw—a not stunningly beautiful kid, kind of unpoised, and a little boney.

"The kid has nothing," he said. "Her eyes are too old. She doesn't have the face of a kid." But Cowdin had left orders, and the contract was ready.

Elizabeth was more sensitive to people than her mother was. She sensed Kelley's animosity. "The casting director instantly disliked me," she said later. Now began a struggle of wills between mother and daughter. Mother liked Universal; the smaller studio might give Elizabeth a better break. Besides —M.G.M. was offering $100 a week, and Universal was offering $200! Daughter like M.G.M.; it was bigger, and the men there were nice to her. Besides, Kelley hated her.

In the event, Elizabeth's instincts proved to be right and her mother's wrong. The contract at Universal was signed, and the studio immediately put her to work in a monstrous piece of fluff called *Man or Mouse.*

The plot? A small-town inventor comes up with a pudding containing Vitamin Z, a recipe that will revolutionize dietetics everywhere. When rivals try to badmouth the formula, the inventor exposes them, becomes mayor of the town, and . . .

First day on the set started the legend of Elizabeth Taylor. The camerman took one look at her and told her to go back to makeup. "You've got too much gook on your eyelashes, honey. Have them take it off."

But Elizabeth had not even been to makeup. "That's just me," she told the cameraman.

Elizabeth was teamed with a somewhat aging juvenile from the Our Gang comedies named Carl "Alfalfa" Switzer. She worked three days on the picture, "running around and shooting rubber bands at ladies' bottoms," as she remembered it. She also sang an off-key duet with Switzer, supposedly for laughs. Switzer's specialty was singing so far off key he sounded sick.

The picture was released under the title *There's One Born Every Minute,* and died a merciful death after a short run. Switzer, incidentally, continued on in movies for some years, then quit, and was killed mysteriously in 1959 in a still unsolved gun brawl.

Universal didn't know what to do with Elizabeth. They made her practice singing every day, but she didn't improve much. No more pictures came up. At the end of the year, the studio dropped her option. But she had been bitten by the acting bug. She and her mother made the rounds. The Cazalets in England had given Sara a letter of introduction to Hedda Hopper, who, along with Louella Parsons and Sheilah Graham, was one of the reigning practitioners of Tinseltown belles lettres—gossip columnists to the uninitiated.

Hopper listened to Elizabeth sing. The ex-trouper shook her head. Not only could Elizabeth not carry a tune, she didn't project either. The clear implication was for both Taylors to forget films for Elizabeth.

The problem was in Hollywood's misconception of child stars during that pre-war era. There were two clichés: the goo-goo girl with bouncing curls and treacle grin as popularized by Shirley Temple; the surly fun-loving evil little brat who went around "shooting rubber bands at ladies' bottoms," as popularized by Margaret O'Brien.

Sound was still a toy the studios had not quite understood or mastered. Naturally, all little girls *had* to sing—it was part of their persona. Elizabeth Taylor got stuck in the flypaper of the fad. By the time Universal forced her to practice every day, she had become a lousy singer who sang from the book rather than from the heart. Elizabeth was neither a studio brat *nor* a singer; ergo, she was not usable.

By now Francis Taylor had moved his art gallery from the Hollywood location to a new one in the Beverly Hills Hotel. Hollywood was an arid desert for fine art, even though there were a few bigwigs and true aristocrats who had taste. Beverly Hills was Snob City, and the Beverly Hills Hotel, just off the trotting lane along Sunset Boulevard, was Snob Center. The Taylor gallery was to remain there until he closed up shop entirely years later.

To be closer to his work, Taylor shopped around for real estate in Beverly Hills, and settled on a place on Elm Drive. It was a pretentious, fake-Mediterranean stucco with a red-tiled roof, typically West Coast fraudulent, but spacious and comfortable to live in. There the Taylors moved, and Howard and Elizabeth were enrolled in Hawthorne School, one of the several grammar schools run by the Beverly Hills school system—grades one through eight.

Once again world events intruded. First, Hitler had driven the Taylors from England to Tinseltown. Now a Japanese war lord named Tojo was preparing another disaster. When Pearl Harbor was bombed on December 7, 1941, a combination of disbelief, apprehension, and total panic seized the West Coast from Tiajuana to the Strait of Juan de Fuca. Blackouts became the way of life. Nisei (American-born Japanese) were rounded up into concentration camps. It was total war.

One submarine did surface somewhere off the coast of Santa Barbara, took a look at the coastline, and then vanished forever. But the populace immediately sprang into action. Civilians were appointed air-raid wardens to patrol areas and herd people into their homes during air raids that never came. Francis Taylor was one. So were many

Hollywood producers, executives, and creative artists.

Hollywood's output was changing, too. The Battle of Britain had seized the public fancy. It was time to begin toughening up the American people. Anglophobes were hard to find in 1941. Churchill's courage and strong will *needed* adulation. The movies obliged.

One night Francis Taylor was patrolling Elm Drive when he happened to meet another air-raid warden he had become acquainted with at a meeting of wardens. His name was Sam Marx. Marx was a producer at M.G.M., now wrestling with casting problems on a new picture scheduled to build up Anglo-American good will. As they were talking, a third warden, Dave Huyler, strolled up.

"How's your picture, *Lassie Come Home*, getting on, Sam?" Huyler asked Marx.

"We're having trouble finding a little English girl to play opposite Roddy McDowall."

Huyler looked at Taylor, then turned back to Marx. "Have you ever seen Taylor's little girl? She's a honey—and she was born and raised in England."

Marx had never seen Elizabeth. He invited Taylor to bring her over the next day—Sunday—to his house. When Taylor told Sara about Marx's invitation, the two of them conferred with Elizabeth. Taylor had been annoyed at the Universal fiasco. He felt that it had hurt Elizabeth, and he didn't want to see her suffer any more. Besides, the movie business was not his idea of Paradise.

Sara was much more sanguine. She knew the scene for what it was; she had been *in* it. After some discussion, they decided to let the answer rest with Elizabeth. They found that her first brush with Universal had not soured her at all.

Now Sara had another idea. She dug out an old copy of the play in which she had starred, *The Fool,* and handed her the big scene in it. By now it was obvious that Elizabeth was not a singer, but perhaps she might be able to act.

"You read the part of the crippled girl," Sara said. "I'll be Mr. Gilchrist, who has been beaten up by the mob." (It was *that* kind of play.)

Elizabeth read the lines. She was so overpowered by her own feelings, that she ended the scene weeping as she spoke. Through tear-stained eyes she looked at her mother, was astonished to find her weeping too, along with her father.

He shrugged, reluctantly agreeing to let her go see Marx. Next day there was a short meeting at Marx's place. The producer wanted Elizabeth to try out for the part. They had already tried out twenty-five girls and had the part narrowed down to a small handful.

Elizabeth showed up late in the day for the test. She read through the page she was to learn and handed it back. She knew it by heart after one reading. The idea was to do a scene with her grandfather and Lassie, a big collie dog, supposedly on the floor in front of her.

The picture's director, Fred M. Wilcox, played the grandfather, and Elizabeth pretended to stroke Lassie as she talked to him. Of course, she had lived for years in her own fantasy-land of animals and made-up people. She had absolutely no trouble in doing the bit.

When she was through Wilcox looked at Marx.

"I didn't expect much from Elizabeth," Marx admitted later. "We had five other girls whom we were considering. We practically had selected one. But the moment Elizabeth entered, there was a complete eclipse of all the others. She was stunning, dazzling. Her voice was charming and she had no self-consciousness whatsoever."

The test came out even better than director or producer thought it would.

"When we looked at it the next day, we knew we had a find," Marx said, probably the understatement of his career.

"It was a snap for a Walter-Mittying dog lover," Elizabeth wrote in her memoirs. (Walter Mitty was a character in a James Thurber short story who lived his life imagining himself in dramatic situations.)

To say that *Lassie Come Home* was a hit is simply to ignore the fact that not only did it do well in the theaters of the time, but it spawned several clones later on, and a long-lasting television series that ran through about a dozen dogs. The first Lassie, incidentally, was a male.

Interestingly enough, most people today think of Lassie as an American dog, living in some unnamed portion of the midwest or far west. Lassie is really as Scottish as her name implies. The product of the facile pen of Eric Knight, the story takes place in Scotland, where the faithful dog is ripped from the hands of her young master, endures countless desecrations at the hands of strangers, and escapes to make her way over the trackless wastes of the Highlands and Lowlands to her home!

Knight lifted the central plot of Jack London's

Call of the Wild as the skeleton of his story, but nobody could read London's book without a slight clutch at the heartstrings. Knight changed the scenery to Scotland and the characters from Gold Rush bruisers to crusty old Scots types. Half the British community in Hollywood played in the picture: Dame May Whitty, Ben Webster, Edmund Gwenn, Elsa Lanchester, Donald Crisp, Nigel Bruce—and Roddy McDowall, fresh from *How Green Was My Valley*.

Elizabeth and McDowall hit it off remarkably well, and the two of them were to remain close throughout their lives. "The film is notable to me," she wrote, "mainly because I met its star, a little boy named Roddy McDowall who is now just about my oldest friend—and really the perfect friend. He makes you feel that you're terribly dear to him and even that maybe you're a dear person."

The public and critics discovered not only Lassie but Elizabeth Taylor as well. The *Hollywood Reporter* said: "Elizabeth Taylor looks like a comer." The *Los Angeles Herald-Examiner:* "Little Elizabeth Taylor is lovely."

Unlike Universal, M.G.M. knew what to do with Elizabeth Taylor. The studio put her in role after role, and even lent her out to other studios for work.

Her second picture was a very small bit part in *Jane Eyre*, the Charlotte Brontë Gothic about Mr. Rochester and a strange disembodied "ghost" in the attic. Orson Welles was Mr. Rochester; Joan Fontaine Jane Eyre, with a script by Aldous Huxley, John Houseman, and Robert Stevenson.

(What a crew of professionals!)

Elizabeth Taylor was lent to Twentieth-Century Fox in 1943 for that job. She played Helen Burns, a classmate of the young Jane Eyre, who was played by Peggy Ann Garner.

Elizabeth arouses the ire of the school's sadistic headmaster, Henry Daniell, who cuts off her hair and then forces both Elizabeth and Peggy to endure a work detail in the freezing rain. Elizabeth dies of pneumonia. She received no screen credit.

Next she played a bit part at M.G.M. in the *White Cliffs of Dover,* Clarence Brown's Anglophiliac version of the Alice Duer Miller poem. It was a real tear-jerker about Hitler and invasion and all that. Once again she was featured with Roddy McDowall, this time as a neighbor girl in love with Roddy, who was Irene Dunne's son.

Anglophilia was still in vogue in 1943, even though the war effort was now in high gear and seemed to be acquiring enough muscle to push back at the Nazi juggernaut. The trouble was, there weren't really enough heroic English novels to make into pictures. And so the studios began reaching back into the files.

In 1935, Enid Bagnold had written an essentially soapy little story about a girl rider who wins a horse in a raffle and trains him for the Grand National Steeplechase—riding him in disguise as a boy to win! How hokey can you get?

The girl's name is Velvet Brown. And because Velvet wins the Steeplechase, she becomes "National" Velvet—get it? Nobody else ever did understand the title. But it didn't matter. The marvelous linking of Elizabeth Taylor and a real horse called King Charles, whose grandsire was the famous Man O'War, put the picture over. And *National Velvet* became the vehicle that made Elizabeth Taylor a star.

She was twelve years old when the property—as they called the script of *National Velvet,* written by Theodore Reeves and Helen Deutsch—wound up at M.G.M. after being considered for such stars as Katharine Hepburn (at R.K.O.), Margaret Sullavan (at M.G.M.), and Spencer Tracy as the father (at M.G.M.). But before anything could be realized, Paramount snatched up the rights. Failing to get a cast together, Paramount then sold the property to M.G.M. in 1937.

Meanwhile, Pandro S. Berman, who had originally thought of Hepburn in the role while at R.K.O., moved to M.G.M., where he was magically reunited with the property, but without the services of Hepburn. Casting difficulties immediately arose. What he needed was an actress who spoke with a British accent and could also ride a horse. Hepburn could ride, but she was, well—Hepburn. Sullavan would have to be dubbed. And who would ride for her?

Elizabeth Taylor knew the book very well. "It was my favorite book," she said. Besides that, she knew she was a good rider. She had proved it in *Lassie* when in a scene she rode up to Nigel Bruce. The shot was cut from the movie. The horse had reared but she had controlled him expertly. The technicians knew how skilled she was in the saddle.

Mickey Rooney was already cast as the jockey who helps Velvet train the horse—called The Pi in

the film (short for "The Pirate"). And there was
talk about Elizabeth as Velvet. But when Berman
called her in to measure her height against
Rooney's, he saw that she was still tiny.

"You're too small," he said. "We want to start
in three months. You should be at least three inches taller."

"I will grow, Mr. Berman. I will grow *three inches.*"

And she did.

At least, that's the story the publicity department at M.G.M. dreamed up. To a degree, Elizabeth believed it too. "I was absolutely determined," she said. "I started riding every morning for an hour and a half before school." And she
ate two hamburger patties, two fried eggs, and a
great big mound of hashed brown potatoes, plus a
bunch of dollar pancakes for breakfast every day.

For lunch she ate steaks and salads, then she'd
swim and do stretching exercises.

And that's how she grew three inches. So much
for *her* version.

There's a third version of the story that makes a
bit more sense. It involves an important man in
Elizabeth's life: a no-nonsense actor's agent named
Jules Goldstone, who took charge of her career
about this time to get her out of bit parts and into
the big time with *National Velvet.* It was apparently
he who made the deal with Berman.

"She *had* the part," Berman said. "She was under contract. We had Mickey Rooney lined up. *I*
made the decision to wait two years. *I* decided that
when she reached a certain height we'd make the
picture. And we did."

To train for her steeplechasing, Elizabeth was given lessons every day at the Riviera Country Club by Snowy Baker, an Australian polo player. There she rode over the course of eight brush jumps four times an hour—forty jumps. She rode an hour every morning before school and then again in the afternoon.

It was there that she found King Charles. He was owned by a Miss Charles, who had a private stable of race horses at Riviera. And it was King Charles who eventually became The Pi in the picture.

Reminiscent of her earlier affection for animals —and in particular her first horse, Betty—Elizabeth took to going out to the stable where King Charles was kept and talking to him. However, all this unscheduled rehearsing and riding exercise set the teeth of the studio brass on edge. When they discovered that she was taking the horse over the steeplechase every day, they grounded her until the picture started.

Besides Mickey Rooney, Elizabeth acted with Donald Crisp again, Anne Revere, as her mother, Angela Lansbury and Juanita Quigley as her sisters, and Jack "Butch" Jenkins as her brother. Reginald Owen and Arthur Treacher were also featured.

It's a simple story, with horse and girl at its core. But there's more to it than simply the training of the horse by Rooney and the girl's efforts to enter The Pi in the National Steeplechase. There's a genuine feeling established between the girl and the horse—and between the girl and the members of her family, plus the relationship between her and the jockey.

When the picture opened in February 1945 the critics were absolutely stunned. James Agee: "I have been choked with the peculiar sort of adoration I might have felt if we were both in the same grade of primary school." And, "She and the picture are wonderful, and I hardly know or care whether she can act or not."

"In *National Velvet*," wrote *Variety*, the trade journal of the industry, "Metro has one of the top b.o. clicks of the year. It's a horse picture with wide general appeal, a potent draw for femme and juve attendance, in particular. The production also focuses attention on a new dramatic find—moppet Elizabeth Taylor, who plays Velvet."

And Eileen Creelman in the *New York Sun:* "That beautiful child of *Lassie Come Home,* a dark-haired, blue-eyed girl named Elizabeth Taylor, plays the dreamy Velvet and makes her one of the screen's most lovable characters."

"It makes a star of twelve-year-old Elizabeth Taylor," said *Pic Magazine,* an imitation-*Life* picture magazine of the era.

Kate Cameron in the *New York Daily News* noticed another particularly important point: "Elizabeth is admirably suited to the role. She gives a glowing performance that actually overshadows her vis-à-vis Mickey Rooney, who is one of Hollywood's prime scene-stealers."

Elizabeth's impact was summed up much later by Pauline Kael, in a review of the 1940s from the vantage point of the 1960s:

"The high point in Elizabeth Taylor's acting career came when she was twelve: under Clarence Brown's direction, she gave her best performance to date as Velvet Brown, the heroine of Enid Bagnold's account of a little girl's sublime folly. Quite possibly the role coincided with the child's own animal-centered universe.

"In lots of ways *National Velvet* isn't a very good movie, but it has a rare and memorable quality. It's one of the most *likable* movies of all time."

But the capper for Elizabeth took place on her thirteenth birthday. For a present, the studio gave her King Charles.

"Jeepers!" screamed Elizabeth Taylor, and burst into tears.

Later on, when Pandro S. Berman and Elizabeth Taylor were "reunited," as they say, on the film *Butterfield 8,* her last for M.G.M., Elizabeth started out their reunion by remarking:

"Aren't you the guy that gave me the horse after *National Velvet*?"

Berman admitted that he was. "Yes, I am afraid that I am."

"You son of a bitch!" burst out Elizabeth Taylor, who by that time had learned to swear like a trouper. "I'm still paying for feed for that goddamned horse!"

What really made *National Velvet* so good was Elizabeth's own background, her familiarity not only with England, but with horses as well, for animals play a much greater and more sentimental part in the English mind than in the American mind. Her rapport with the horse, and her ability to control him in the scenes she played came across on the screen with a startling intensity.

By the time she was through playing the role, she was thinking and acting pretty much the way Velvet Brown would act. A strange thing was happening. Elizabeth Taylor had created a role for herself, had made a motion picture, and then had begun to play that role in real life from that day on. Picture by picture she added to her own dimension as a person, as well as an actress.

It was a strange way to grow up—through another person's creativity. But it seemed to work. Of course, there could be no substitute for the real experience of growing up. Her whole early life was strictly make-believe, with her lines written for her, her actions laid out for her, her role in life already established from the outside.

She had no true role models, only the empty qualities of morality and ethics that the movies projected. No wonder she cried out with joy when the studio gave her a horse—and then bitched about the reality of the ownership some sixteen years later.

CHAPTER THREE
Sudden Siren

The returns were in, and one fact was abundantly clear: Elizabeth Taylor was a star. But she was a star at the awkward age of thirteen. The problem was how to get her through the bad years during puberty and into adulthood without losing her audience. M.G.M.'s answer to the problem was to put her in a string of pictures that really didn't advance her career any but that gave her plenty of exposure:

Courage of Lassie, a spin-off of *Lassie Come Home*.

Cynthia, a soapy Viña Delmar play.

Life with Father, a costume play.

A Date with Judy, movie out of radio series. (loaned out to Warner Brothers for this)

Julia Misbehaves, an adaptation of Margery Sharp's *The Nutmeg Tree*.

Little Women, a remake of the 1933 Hepburn movie.

Meanwhile, during the "in-between" years, her personal life was a far different proposition from her early years in Beverly Hills before she became a child film prodigy. The last vestiges of normal life vanished shortly after she had signed with M.G.M.

Up to that time she had been going to public school with her brother Howard at Hawthorne School in Beverly Hills. However, shortly after *Lassie Come Home* was released, the principal at Hawthorne decided that her presence in class was too disruptive for her to remain. She called in Sara and told her that the children were spending most of their time *staring* at Elizabeth rather than concentrating on their work. Sara was advised to transfer her out of the public school system to the studio school at M.G.M.

California law required that children of school age must attend school for at least three hours daily, even if they were in costume and make-up. When Elizabeth was working on a picture, she was accompanied on the set by a tutor—one of the teachers who was with her for the required three hours of study.

When Elizabeth was duly transferred to the studio school, located in Irving Thalberg's old bungalow on the lot—a school to which Elizabeth sometimes referred so sardonically as "M.G.M. University"—she was assigned to a tutor-teacher named Mrs. Birdina Anderson.

"We were annoyed about it," said Sara, "but there was nothing we could do." Elizabeth was in the sixth grade. She would stay at M.G.M. U. until she had finished the twelfth. In addition to her tutor, Elizabeth also had a "guardian" along when she was working. Her guardian was Sara, appropriately enough, who was paid $250 a month by the studio—the going rate for "studio mothers." Starting out at $200 a week, Elizabeth gradually made more and more money, reaching $1,000 a week in 1949, and rising to $1,500 in 1950, and so on.

Elizabeth was a reserved girl in school. She was, in the words of one M.G.M. observer, a "quiet child, very much under the mother's thumb—and her mother, then as later, idolized her." By the time she had gone through her twelfth year, she had achieved a good solid B average—perhaps a B + . An assessment of her work for those years was that she was a "good student, very good in art, with a flair for writing."

One homework project turned out to be an unexpected boon for the publicity department. Elizabeth had been told to write a paper on one of her animals. She did a piece on her chipmunk, Nibbles, and entitled it *Nibbles and Me*. She was only thirteen when she wrote the paper, but the project took on enormous dimensions. It developed into a 77-page thesis—a book, really.

When Andy—Mrs. Birdina Anderson—sent it to the publicity department, they were ecstatic. After a bit of pruning and paring, the manuscript was sent to Duell, Sloan and Pearce, which published it in its entirety.

Sara Taylor was much more than a guardian and studio mother. She was Elizabeth's dramatic coach as well. She was there at every bit of filming. While Elizabeth was emoting, she would carefully watch her mother for signals. For example, if Sara thought Elizabeth's voice was getting too high, she would put her hand on her own stomach, meaning

for Elizabeth to bring her voice *down*. If Elizabeth
seemed to be performing a bit woodenly, Sara
would put her hand to her heart, meaning to give it
a little more soul. If Elizabeth simply started walking through the role too mechanically, Sara would
put her finger to her head, meaning for Elizabeth
to *think* about what she was saying and doing. If
Elizabeth was too dour or sullen, Sara would put a
finger to her cheek, meaning to smile more. And if
Elizabeth started to ham it up too much, Sara
would put a finger to her neck, meaning that she
was "up to here" in schmaltz and not to go under
completely.

The stress on Elizabeth's career was causing
some cracks to appear in the Taylor family solidar-
ity. The house on Elm Drive began to resemble a
mausoleum to Elizabeth. "There were from six to
twelve photographs of her in each room, sometimes posed alone, sometimes posed beside her
mother: You'd never have known there was a Taylor male around," one friend said.

In fact, a lot of the time, there *wasn't* a Taylor
male around.

"Daddy and Howard went fishing in Wisconsin
with Uncle Howard," was the way Sara Taylor
noted it in her magazine memoirs published by the
Ladies Home Journal in 1954. But that was a eu-
phemistic way of getting at the real problem. The
truth was, the Taylor family was splitting up—
right in the middle, females on one side and males
on the other.

What had happened was a very familiar sight in
Hollywood. As Francis Taylor had receded into
the background after his daughter's entry into the
movies, Sara Taylor had come forward, reentering

show business with her daughter. She was rejuvenated by the change. Sara took off pounds and tinted her hair.

In effect, she became a living extension of her daughter. Mother and daughter were with each other every waking moment—at M.G.M. school, shopping in Beverly Hills, on the set. Even at press conferences, Sara would automatically give answers to questions asked Elizabeth.

Sara drove Elizabeth to work every morning and home again at night. Family conversation at the dinner table revolved around studio gossip and shop talk between Elizabeth and Sara.

Francis Taylor and Howard munched their food in silence.

Howard was in Beverly Hills High School and had his own set of friends. He kept his personal life to himself. Occasionally Sara would reproach him for not getting into the movie business himself. His mane of curly hair and blue eyes not unlike Elizabeth's made him look like a Greek god, Hollywood-style. He was as handsome as ever. Producers who had worked with Elizabeth constantly approached him with film offers.

Jules Goldstone was now handling Elizabeth's career; he had made her a star by clinching the part of Velvet Brown for her. Now he wanted to mold Howard. He worked up a screen test at Universal Pictures. When Goldstone told Howard about it, he finally broke down and said he would meet Goldstone at the appointed time for the test.

Howard appeared as promised. Goldstone froze. Universal was not amused. Howard had gone to a barber and had his head shaved to the skull, a handsome Kojak long before his time.

"That was the end of his movie career," sighed Goldstone.

Elizabeth saw it differently. "How I admired Howard's disdain for the movies!" she later admitted.

All the attention focused on Elizabeth and Sara finally got to Francis Taylor, who spent most of his time sitting in his art gallery being ignored by the very people who worked so hard to please his daughter and wife. To cap all this, Sara was so close to the power structure in the industry that she was bound to be affected. Sure enough, she managed to fall for one of the glamorous directors working on one of her daughter's pictures.

Michael Curtiz was a suave, sophisticated, and knowledgeable man, the director who had made *Casablanca* with Humphrey Bogart and Ingrid Bergman, and *Mildred Pierce* with Joan Crawford, along with a long string of successes. The swinging Hungarian was assigned to *Life with Father,* in which Elizabeth played Mary, and Sara began to be seen going places with him.

The romance soon broke up, as most like that do. But not before Francis had had it; he and Sara formally separated. Howard went along with his father. They spent some time in other parts of the country.

His leaving didn't affect Elizabeth much at all. She had several surrogate fathers at the studio. M.G.M. was her real family by then.

She once said: "I looked on Benny Thau [one of the top brass] and Jules Goldstone as my two fathers, and I went to them for help and for advice."

Help and advice were two things Elizabeth Taylor began to need at this point in her life. She was just past fourteen when quite suddenly the little girl who talked to animals and wrote stories about chipmunks simply vanished. Quickly and spectacularly the adolescent became a woman, metamorphosing quickly from a moppet to a siren, with no in-between period of pimples and boils.

She developed a thirty-seven inch bust that was as spectacular in its way as her face and eyes. It was a time of breast fixation in America. The big bosom was the rage. Not to touch, not to fondle, not even to tweak, but simply to ogle and admire.

Such obvious excitement over a simple mammalian appurtenance is difficult to picture in these days of unisex views, with their equal pay, equal jobs, and equal shapes. Today thirty-seven inches around the chest isn't the invitation to fun and games—and total ecstasy—that it was in those long-gone times.

Anyway, one day Elizabeth Taylor walked into the studio commissary and almost every man there froze in position, fork halfway to mouth, coffee cup in hand, or chocolate mousse suspended in air —as this woman, wearing a swinging full skirt, a tightly clenched belt around her narrow waist, and an extremely low-cut peasant blouse clinging to an enormous pair of extremely well-developed breasts, sauntered by.

One unbelieving M.G.M. executive later said: "Her bosom bounced, she had that look in her eye —and every man at the studio had a new look in his eye, too."

So did every woman. Ann Straus, head of the

studio picture gallery, recalled that she had to watch Elizabeth carefully, because if she wasn't held in check, she would always dress in off-the-shoulder blouses to enhance the bounce of her thirty-sevens.

Straus felt that she resembled a "Joan Crawford hussy" rather than a sexually attractive female. Elizabeth was doing more than dressing up in revealing costumes. She was experimenting with lipstick, too, and other kinds of make-up. What she wanted, and didn't get, were dates with boys of her own age.

A normal teen-age life style was impossible in the studio atmosphere. She sat around, one biographer wrote, "went to school, drew her weekly wage, and wrote morbid poetry that reflected her despair." And that brought on experimentation with off-the-shoulder gowns and daily shows of walking across the commissary to freeze all Culver City males into frustrated immobility.

Her love life was lousy. She was concerned about her sex appeal. When her father and brother did eventually return to the fold after a half year's sabbatical, she conned her brother into blind dates with friends from high school. No go. Howard's friends were three years older than she was.

Even when Roddy McDowall was given a birthday party by a fan magazine, Elizabeth couldn't find a date. She finally went to it with Bill Lyon, a studio publicity flak.

"They both had a wonderful time," Sara related. Elizabeth's opinion is not known.

In desperation Elizabeth finally formed a club with Betty Sullivan, columnist Ed Sullivan's daughter. It was called the Single Lonely Obliging Babes—the "SLOB Club."

Sara finally worked out a solution. She somehow got Marshall Thompson, a juvenile actor at M.G.M., to take Elizabeth out on a date. He did so. He took her to a picture, then to an ice-cream parlor for a chocolate sundae, and on the way home—*he kissed her!*

A milestone in the life of Elizabeth Taylor was passed.

From today's point of view, such a milestone is, of course, a ridiculous joke. But it was no such thing in those up-tight neo-Victorian days. "The first kiss" was also a problem for the entire hierarchy of Metro-Goldwyn-Mayer Studios.

The front office burned the midnight oil worrying about it. How the hell could they get this big-busted, beautiful, ravishing young virgin legally and tastefully *through* her first kiss?

Larger issues have troubled heads of state, but none were so carefully dissected and mulled over than the case of Elizabeth Taylor's first screen kiss. But first let's take a look at what she had been doing professionally since her brilliant debut in *National Velvet.*

Her next film was *Courage of Lassie,* a kind of reprise of *Lassie Come Home.* In it, she got top billing as star. Even though the title mentions a Lassie, the film does not star Lassie. The dog in the picture is named Bill. In fact, the story takes place not in England, where Lassie came from, but in the western United States—the state of Washington, to be exact.

The collie Bill is accidentally shot by a couple of

kids hunting birds, and Elizabeth finds him, nursing him back to health. One day when he's rounding up sheep, he is hit by a car, and becomes involved in a series of misadventures that lead him into combat where he serves against the Japanese! War turns Bill vicious. When Elizabeth—her name is Kathie Merrick in the movie—finds Bill again he attacks her. The dog has become a sheep-killer, breaking into pens and slashing them up. She has to plead his case to save him from being killed by the ranchers. Shell-shock, you know.

Courage of Bill—uh—*Courage of Lassie* proved to be a walk-through for Elizabeth. The critics shrugged. "Lassie walks off with all the acting honors, which is as it should be," wrote Joe Pihodna in the *New York Herald Tribune,* ignoring the fact that Lassie wasn't even in the picture.

"Elizabeth Taylor is refreshingly natural as Lassie's devoted owner," wrote A.H. Weiler in the *New York Times.* Wanda Hale in the *New York Daily News* warned her readers that the story was unreal and "slightly tedious." However, "Elizabeth Taylor, very beautiful and charmingly sincere, has the leading role as Bill's devoted mistress."

It was between the filming of *Courage of Lassie* and *Cynthia,* her next vehicle, that Elizabeth had her big run-in with Louis B. Mayer. The studio head was an amazing combination of genius, ruthlessness, excitability, and volatility. He loved to punch anyone who annoyed him—really punch, with his fist.

But Mayer considered himself anything but a power-mad mogul. It had been said around Hollywood that the letters M.G.M. stood for Mayer's-

Gang-Mispochen, fractured Yiddish for "Mayer's whole family." And he was the father.

He used to annoy star William Haines by throwing his arms around Haines's shoulders, and crying: "Oh, my son. I never had a son. I always wanted a son." Haines finally found a way to stop the maudlin act. He would burst into tears himself. "He was a dyed-in-the-wool son of a bitch," Haines said.

Robert Taylor once bearded the lion in his den to ask for a raise. He got the full monologue from Mayer. A friend asked him later if he got the raise.

"No," said Taylor. "But I got a father!"

"I thought he was a beast," Elizabeth said of him. "He was inhuman. He used his power over people to such a degree that he became not a man but an instrument of power."

The publicity mill had ground out a story that Metro had bought a property called *Salley in Her Alley* for Elizabeth. It was about a Cockney girl. Sara and Elizabeth wanted to know more about it because the release had mentioned singing and dancing. They asked for an appointment with Mayer to discuss training for it.

Apparently Mayer knew little about the project. He sat behind his big white oak desk in an office that Elizabeth said looked like Mussolini's with a mile of white carpet in front of it, and listened to what Sara had to say about the property. Then he blew his top. He turned white with anger and burst out swearing. Then he got up and banged on the desk, shaking with rage. Out poured every four-letter word in the language, and possibly a few others.

A cleaned-up version of the tirade appeared in

Elizabeth's memoirs, but the original must have gone like this:

"You're so goddamned fucking stupid you wouldn't even know what day of the week it is," he told Sara. "Don't try to meddle into my affairs. Don't try to tell me how to make motion pictures. I took you out of the gutter!"

Sara was reduced to quivering silence, but not Elizabeth. She jumped up, screaming: "Don't you dare to speak to my mother like that. You and your studio can both go to hell!"

She rushed out of the office, with Mayer fuming behind his oak revetment. Her mother calmed Mayer down, and then followed her out. Although she was advised to apologize to him, she never did.

Salley in her Alley, or *Introduction to Sally* as it was also called, never saw the light of day. Mayer's days at M.G.M. were numbered. Dore Schary arrived at M.G.M. in July, 1948, and only a little over three years from that date the man who started M.G.M. was out.

Elizabeth's next movie was *Cynthia,* an adaptation of a play called *The Rich Full Life.* The play, a non-success on Broadway, turned out to be a non-success at Metro. But the big pitch in the advertising was "Her First Kiss"! Her first screen kiss was given to her by an unlikely actor named James Lydon—who he?—and the big kiss occurred in a scene on the doorstep.

The mawkish plot revolved around a sickly teenager—Taylor!—whose big achievement in the movie was to revolt against her overprotective parents and go to a school prom.

Her first screen kiss almost coincided with her first real kiss. "Marshall gave me my first kiss—

two days before I was first kissed in *Cynthia*," she said.

Her second screen kiss came while she was 15, in *Julia Misbehaves*—and the man who gave her that kiss was Peter Lawford, later to be brother-in-law to the President of the United States (Jack Kennedy), and Charlie the Seal in the famed Hollywood Rat Pack. "Peter to me was the last word in sophistication," she said. "He was terribly handsome, and I had a tremendous crush on him. I became so flustered when he kissed me that I got bright red, while the crew went into hysterics."

Julia Misbehaves was an adaptation of Margery Sharp's *The Nutmeg Tree*, starring Greer Garson, Walter Pidgeon, Cesar Romero, and Lawford. Elizabeth played Garson's daughter in the tearjerker about a music-hall actress separated from her high-society husband and her misadventures in trying to get her daughter married to the right man. The critics liked Elizabeth.

"The picture receives a most valuable decoration in the presence of Elizabeth Taylor, former child star, who has developed into one of the cinema's reigning queens of beauty and talent. She plays Julia's daughter with both sincerity and charm," wrote Otis L. Guernsey, Jr., for the *New York Herald Tribune*.

"Elizabeth Taylor is the daughter who upsets her rich relatives when she elopes with an eager painter, elegantly portrayed by Peter Lawford. They shape up as a strong team of juves." That was *Variety*'s appraisal.

And *Time* with a no-no: "Elizabeth Taylor who is just beginning to move into grown-up roles, is one of the loveliest girls in movies; but here she is made-up and hair-done and directed into tired, tiresome conventional prettiness."

In between her two screen kisses, Elizabeth played in a bunch of high budget pictures. One was a loan-out to Warner Brothers. *Life with Father* was an adaptation from the Howard Lindsay and Russell Crouse play, starring William Powell, Irene Dunne, and Edmund Gwenn. The cast was large, and very professional. But even with all that competition, Elizabeth was noticed.

"Elizabeth Taylor is sweetly feminine," said *Variety*. "Elizabeth Taylor is alternately kittenish, silly and coquettish, as she is romantically involved with Clarence, Jr." said *The Film Daily*. The *Los Angeles Times:* "Lovely Elizabeth Taylor as the oldest boy's sweetie is charming and clever."

It will be remembered that it was during the filming of *Life with Father* that Sara Taylor had her fling with Michael Curtiz. "Elizabeth is the most promising dramatic ingenue in years," Curtiz said, and tried to persuade the studio to borrow her again to play in *Green Mansions*—but it was unfortunately a property of M.G.M. M.G.M. wouldn't lend her out for it; nor did the studio make it with Elizabeth Taylor. Audrey Hepburn finally became Rima the Bird Girl later in 1959 to thundering indifference.

Next came an M.G.M. teen-age flick called *A Date with Judy*, a movie version of a popular radio serial. In this one Elizabeth played with Jane Powell, a juvenile called Scotty Beckett, and Robert Stack, later to be Eliot "Stoneface" Ness in TV's *The Untouchables*. A very light piece of fluff, it did offer one rather surprising and interesting new facet to Elizabeth Taylor's talent:

"The big surprise in *A Date with Judy*," wrote Otis L. Guernsey, Jr., of the *New York Herald Tribune*, "is Elizabeth Taylor as the petulant, dark-eyed banker's daughter. The erstwhile child star of *National Velvet* and other films has been touched by Metro's magic wand and turned into a real, 14-carat, 100-proof siren with a whole new career opening in front of her. Judging from this picture, Hedy Lamarr had better watch out, with Miss Taylor coming along."

After *Julia Misbehaves*, M.G.M. dusted off Louisa Mae Alcott's *Little Women* for another try. It had just been made in 1933 by R.K.O., with Katharine Hepburn. This new version starred June Allyson in Hepburn's role, Margaret O'Brien in the Jean Parker role, Janet Leigh in the Frances Dee role, and Elizabeth Taylor in the Joan Bennett role.

"Elizabeth Taylor is appropriately trivial and attractive as Amy," said *Newsweek*. Bosley Crowther in the *New York Times* said that "As Amy, Elizabeth Taylor is appropriately full of artifice. . . ." "Elizabeth Taylor is lovely and properly spoiled in the part of Amy," wrote Howard Barnes in the *New York Herald Tribune*.

Elizabeth Taylor played the role in a blonde wig, and seemed to get by with it. The picture was not as good as the 1933 version, but it won four Oscars for the set designers.

Next on the list was *Conspirator*, a picture in which Elizabeth was to play her first adult role opposite Robert Taylor. But her personal life was beginning to take on all the dramatic and exciting aspects of her professional life.

CHAPTER FOUR
The First Forever

In February, 1948, Elizabeth Taylor celebrated her sixteenth birthday on the set of *Julia Misbehaves,* with Greer Garson, Walter Pidgeon, and Peter Lawford in attendance. But what was more overwhelming to this girl who was used to being around celebrities every working day was a birthday card from Sara and Francis Taylor, enclosed with a set of gold Cadillac keys. The keys operated a light blue Caddy convertible that she would get in three weeks.

Shortly after the party, the Taylors moved from Beverly Hills to Malibu for the summer. For a time now Elizabeth had managed to avoid the spectacular accidents and illnesses that seemed to pursue her. Now it was Howard's turn. One day as the two of them were riding along the beach a stunting airplane swooped down and scared Howard's horse. The horse reared and threw him headlong onto the sand, knocking him unconscious. Elizabeth had been following and rounded a turn to see him lying face down in the surf.

She jumped off her horse and rushed over to drag him out of the water. She sat holding his head up above the water until some boys came up and helped her drag him onto the dry sand.

And then, true to form, a few weeks later it was Elizabeth's turn. A gang of kids were up for a Sunday, riding the waves in rubber rafts. At the end of the Taylor property sharp rocks stuck up out of the water. The kids began to play chicken, to see who could come closest to the rocks without being dashed to death against them.

In the middle of the horseplay the tide changed and a strong rip began working against the main current. Howard's raft overturned, and he managed to swim to shore. But Elizabeth apparently didn't realize the rip tide was so strong; she suddenly found herself being tossed about in huge waves that were rolling in ten or twelve feet high.

On shore Howard saw her, bent backward, being lifted high in the middle of a wave. He plunged into the water to go after her. When he reached her, he grabbed her by the hair and pulled her away from the rocks and through the rip tide. She was unconscious.

By now Francis and Sara were on the beach waiting. Both Howard and his father used artificial respiration on her to bring her back to consciousness.

Life at Malibu wasn't all narrow escapes and frantic mouth-to-mouth resuscitation. There were plenty of beach parties and lots of young boys and girls around. A publicity flak at the studio, Doris Kearns, decided to make some mileage out of Elizabeth's obvious new "maturity," and the fact that she was becoming known as the "most beautiful girl in motion pictures."

She secured an introduction to Glenn Davis, now a lieutenant on leave from the Army. Davis had been a former football great from West Point, co-captain of the Army team with Doc Blanchard. Together this formidable pair had been called the Touchdown Twins. Now in uniform, David was on leave from his tour of duty in the Orient. Not surprisingly, Lieutenant Davis was amenable to associating with Hollywood luminaries, especially pretty ones.

Kearns and her husband, Hubie, brought Davis down to the Taylor place at Malibu on a Saturday afternoon. Elizabeth was playing touch football with a group of kids when Davis arrived. When Sara called her out of the game, she took one look at Davis—whose face was not unknown at that time to the American public—and "volunteered" him for her side.

Good-naturedly, he accepted, and the game went on.

It was obvious that the two of them should be drawn to one another. Each was a professional in his or her own sphere. He took her on dates and everywhere they went the photographers and the reporters were there to ask questions.

"My God," Elizabeth once said, "they think it's a big hot romance."

The Kearnses took Davis and Elizabeth to a *Los Angeles Times* football benefit, and everybody in the stands took a look at Davis and Elizabeth. Instead of cheering the teams on the field, the crowd kept chanting, "We want Davis! We want Davis!"

Elizabeth felt like standing up and shouting, "I'm with Davis! I'm with Davis!"

The press seemed almost as smitten by the couple as Elizabeth was smitten by Davis. Whatever Davis felt, by the end of his tour he had given her his gold football, his All-American sweater, and finally his promise to return to her at the end of his tour of duty in Korea. Remember, that was before the Korean "war"—technically a "conflict"—began.

"We're engaged to be engaged," Elizabeth kidded her friends when they asked. But Davis did eventually purchase an engagement ring for her. Actually, Sara and Francis didn't at all approve of her betrothal at such a young age.

"We thought sixteen too young for marriage, but we never forbade it," Francis said. "There would have been no point in playing the heavy-handed parent, especially when the boy in question was a splendid one. We merely asked Elizabeth to wait."

And wait she did. Working.

Shortly after Davis shipped out to the Orient, Elizabeth and her mother were on the *Queen Mary* bound for London, where she was scheduled to make *Conspirator,* a spy picture with Robert Taylor. *Time* and *Life* duly reported each time Elizabeth Taylor and Robert Taylor were mentioned together that they were "no kin." Robert Taylor's real name was Spangler Arlington Brough—a pretty tough mouthful of molar-breakers to get onto a marquis.

According to the gossip columnists who breathlessly kept count, Elizabeth wrote a letter to her demi-betrothed once a night.

Meanwhile, under the hot lights, she was beginning to give off the effluence of a sultry, magnetic, dynamic sexuality.

"Good Lord!" muttered Victor Saville, her director in London. "Have you any idea what an emotional actress of her age is worth?" He grimaced. "And the best of it is, she doesn't know her power. If she did at that age, she'd be unbearable. I've seen them at sixteen and less when they know it. And you can't say a word because—there's our meal ticket for the next twenty years."

Playing Robert Taylor's wife in the picture, Elizabeth threw herself into the scenes with professional abandon. "They told her to kiss," the star said after one scene, "and she kissed!" Then he paused appreciatively. "The only thing I've had to teach her was to powder down her lips."

Elizabeth had a different reaction. As soon as the scene was finished, she had to leave the set and start her lessons with Andy, her tutor. "How can I concentrate on my education," she wondered, "when Robert Taylor keeps sticking his tongue down my throat?"

Hedda Hopper had it that the love scenes in *Conspirator* were so hot that during one of them Robert Taylor dislocated a vertebra in Elizabeth's back.

However sultry the love scenes were, it wasn't Robert Taylor in whom Elizabeth was interested, but another actor, named Michael Wilding. He was in his late thirties at the time, and a well-known British star who had not yet made any pictures in the United States. His lean, interesting face fascinated Elizabeth.

Wilding was working on another picture, but

Elizabeth would keep seeing him in the studio lunchroom. Sara recalled that in the commissary Wilding used to come over to the table and talk to her and Elizabeth. Sara did notice that Elizabeth's eyes lighted up whenever Wilding was nearby, and said later that if it were not for Glenn Davis, Michael Wilding would be "the man" for her.

Wilding remembered it differently. "Rather than ask the waitress for some salt, she'd walk clear through the commissary to get it from the kitchen, wiggling her hips. Then she'd wiggle her way back."

The picture was finished in September, and the Taylors sailed back to America. M.G.M. wasn't happy with the finished product, and shelved it for about a year. Although Elizabeth was only sixteen, she was playing a twenty-year-old woman in it. Perhaps the studio wanted to wait till she caught up with the role.

Unfortunately, the script was a lackluster thing. From a novel by Humphrey Slater, the screenplay was written by Sally Benson and Gerard Fairlie. Melodramatic, and rather unconvincing on the whole, the picture seemed to be trying to make up its mind between being a thriller and a romance.

Robert Taylor as a traitor simply wouldn't wash all that easily. The *New York Times* took the picture to task not only for the script that had been written in "an uninspired mood," but also for its lugubriousness and the obvious limitations of its stars. Joe Pihodna, of the *New York Herald Tribune,* wrote: "An attempt to make capital of a topical theme has failed dismally on the screen. . . . The hero is handsome and the heroine is pretty. The script merely serves as a background for another screen romance."

Variety disliked the script, but liked Elizabeth. "Elizabeth Taylor is given a big opportunity for an emotional and romantic lead, and comes out with flying colors."

In the States, Elizabeth and her mother were invited to Star Island in Florida by Uncle Howard (Young). There he gave her a big birthday party, with over a hundred people present. One of them was a young man named William D. Pawley, Jr., the vice president of a Florida bus line. Actually, the bus line was owned by his father, who was the millionaire ex-ambassador to Brazil.

Pawley was no slouch. He appeared at Star Island *in his father's boat* and picked up Elizabeth for a cruise. They then went to a dinner dance. After that there were more and more parties. Moonlight, dancing, good food, excitement—it didn't seem to end.

One night Elizabeth had a phone call from Fort Dix. It was Glenn Davis, her Number One Beau, wondering if he could come down to see her. He arrived at the airport which was crowded with photographers and reporters. Davis stayed only a short time with Elizabeth. He took a good hard look at Pawley. It was obvious that he knew which way the wind was blowing.

The football star flew back to California. The gossip columnists had it right. "It's all over with Elizabeth and Glenn Davis, and 'tis said that Elizabeth's mother feels no pain," wrote one. *Time* magazine said: "Suddenly it was all over and Glenn was gone, deftly recovering his fumbled gold football."

And within days Elizabeth was photographed looking at a huge diamond ring that Pawley had bought her. Pawley had the future planned. Elizabeth and he would settle down in Miami and enjoy life. Elizabeth thought it was a wonderful idea . . . at first.

But then M.G.M. scheduled a new picture for her, called *Drink to Me Only,* with Van Johnson. She flew back to the coast to start work. Letters between her and Pawley and long-distance telephone calls helped a little, but not much. It was obvious that the engagement would be short-lived. It was.

Elizabeth was into the filming of *Drink to Me Only* now, which had already been changed to *The Big Hangover,* and Pawley was out of sight and out of mind. In September he flew out to the Coast to get his engagement back on track. Pawley's idea of getting things back on track didn't coincide with Elizabeth's. There was a confrontation. The engagement was dissolved. Pawley flew back to his bus line, a sadder and perhaps luckier man.

Now began one of the oddest courtships of her career. Elizabeth made frequent trips to see her father in his gallery in the Beverly Hills Hotel. To get to the gallery she would pass through the main lobby of the hotel. It was there that she caught the eye of a secret admirer. He saw her going across the lobby one day, and demanded to be introduced.

Her secret admirer was used to getting his way, no matter what he asked. His name was Howard Hughes. At the time the multimillionaire was living in a bungalow at the Beverly Hills Hotel. Ever paranoid, the former owner of R.K.O. pictures, the owner of T.W.A., and the designer of the fighter plane that became the Japanese Zero used to suspect that his phone lines were tapped by enemies. He used the public booth in the hotel lobby, and it was there that he spotted her going to see her father.

Johnny Meyer, Hughes's assistant, was delegated to establish contact. He was used to Hughes's foibles. Like every other red-blooded American, but even more so, Hughes was fixated on the female breast, the bigger the better. "Get me an introduction to that girl," Hughes rasped.

Meyer caught up with her later outside her father's gallery and arranged a meeting in the gallery. Hughes showed up and turned on the charm; he could do it when he wanted to. And money helped. He purchased two paintings from Taylor, and suggested dinner with both father and daughter. It was a standard Hughes ploy: work in to the center from the periphery.

For several weeks Hughes, Elizabeth, her mother and father made strange foursomes at various hot spots around Los Angeles. They were even spotted by gossip columnists in Reno one weekend. But the word was out: no ink on Hughes.

Hughes went mad over Elizabeth. Her cool glacial indifference spurred him on. He would call hostesses and request that he and she be invited to a dinner party. Elizabeth caught on. Every time she was invited anywhere, she would ask cautiously:

"Is Howard Hughes invited? If he is, I'm not coming."

Elizabeth later told the story of their final encounter. "He offered me one million dollars, under-the-table, as he put it, to give him two weeks to coordinate and marry him."

Elizabeth told him: "I'm not in love with you."

Hughes insisted that was only a detail; he needed two weeks' time, that was all. Then, perhaps Elizabeth would fall in love with him.

"I told him one million dollars wouldn't make me fall in love with him. Howard thought everybody had a price tag."

Eventually Hughes surrendered to the inevitable and gave up the chase. But he was a strange bird, a man of many moods and character facets.

Later on, during several personal crises in Elizabeth's life, he was suddenly there with the offer of an airplane to take her somewhere quickly, or money to bail her out of a jam.

After finishing *The Big Hangover* Elizabeth was on loan to Paramount. M.G.M. had run out of properties for her and had answered a call from their crosstown rival. It was a lucky call. Paramount was making *A Place in the Sun,* an adaptation of Theodore Dreiser's masterpiece *An American Tragedy*. She was assigned by director George Stevens to play one third of the triangle composed also of Shelley Winters and Montgomery Clift.

The film became memorable in two specific ways: Elizabeth Taylor received critical acclaim on a professional level, and she gained a lifelong friend on a personal level.

The Dreiser story is essentially the triangle of a young man trying to rise in society and business, a young girl whom he gets pregnant, and a young rich girl whom he wants to marry. His solution is to drown the pregnant girl so he can take the rich girl. In its bare bones the story is based on a true incident in 1906, when Chester Gillette was convicted of murdering Grace Brown so he could marry someone else.

Stevens didn't like the word "tragedy" in Dreiser's title; to him it made the concept too sordid. He changed the outlook to a positive one—Clift's ambition to succeed. The names were changed, too. Dreiser's Clyde Griffiths became George Eastman—that was Clift's part. Sondra Finchely, the lovely rich girl, became Angela Vickers—that was Elizabeth's part. Roberta Alden became Alice Tripp—that was to be played by Shelley Winters.

With the exception of *National Velvet,* the pictures Elizabeth Taylor had made were not particularly complex. But Stevens saw something in her that he liked. Even though criticized for casting her, he had his reasons.

"Liz was a teen-ager, but she had all the emotional capabilities," he said later. "She had the intelligence, sharp as a tack. She was seventeen and she had been an actress all her life. So there was no problem there. The only thing was to prod her a bit into realizing her dramatic potential."

He read her correctly as essentially a lazy person. His procedure was to bully the role out of her.

Clift was another proposition entirely. A seasoned actor who had performed well on the Broadway stage in such hits as *There Shall Be No Night,* he had made *The Search, Red River, The Heiress* and *The Big Lift* in Hollywood with uniform good results. An actor who worked out his scenes with the Method approach of Stanislavsky, he brought great intensity and concentration to a role.

From the beginning, his style of acting impressed Elizabeth. She had never before thought of reaching down into herself to bring out *more* than her director required.

The combination of Stevens and his badgering and Clift and his methodical interpreting was an eye-opener to her. "It was my first real chance to probe myself and Monty helped me," she said later.

She worked hard with him, running their scenes together under the watchful eye of Clift's dramatic coach, Mira Rostova. In itself, the fact that Clift had a drama coach was another surprise to Elizabeth. She was doubly impressed. And Stevens was always in the background, trying to pull more out of them. He made them act each scene out *without* using dialogue, to see if they could evoke the proper emotions in a scene through looks and gestures.

One key scene, when Clift confesses his love for Taylor, was memorable for all three of them. The crucial element of the scene involves their overpowering emotional feeling for one another.

The moment occurs when the two meet at a party. Taylor, frightened by her passion, is startled. She asks Clift, "Are they watching us?" She wants to hide from everyone. She doesn't want her feelings to show. The scene itself is a blockbuster in the movie.

Working so close to Clift through those days, Elizabeth did what she frequently did later on: she fell in love with her leading man. Clift was what is called a "switch-hitter" when it came to sexual preferences. He was homosexual when he wanted to be, and heterosexual when he wanted to be.

Some accounts have it that Elizabeth was perplexed and wounded at his behavior; the truth is, she recognized his problem. It bothered her, of course. But she finally told him that she understood, and that she would always be there whenever he needed her. He was to need her. And she would be there.

Stevens recognized her true feelings for Clift, and made the most of them in the scenes he wrung out of the two of them. In some of the close shots, their emotion is an almost incandescent thing.

At the end of the picture, Clift didn't hang around the set. Instead, he took off for North Carolina to stay with blues singer Libby Holman. They were always good friends. Holman took up with nice strays and mixed-up young people of all kinds.

But the gossip columnists were at work, largely with the invisible help of the studio flak. "Liz Taylor to Wed Montgomery Clift," one of the headlines said. Elizabeth's interest in Clift was a salable commodity that might help sell the picture.

Elizabeth Taylor definitely matured during the making of *A Place in the Sun*. Her professional career improved vastly. The critics were uniformly impressed.

"The success of *A Place in the Sun* is probably attributable to George Stevens, who produced and directed it with workmanlike restraint and without tricks or sociological harangue," wrote the *New York Herald Tribune*. "He has drawn excellent performances from Montgomery Clift, who is thoroughly believable as the young man; Elizabeth Taylor, who is remarkably well cast as the daughter of a wealthy social clan; and Shelley Winters, who is particularly moving in the role of the unwanted sweetheart."

Time said: "Actress Taylor plays with a tenderness and intensity that may surprise even her warmest fans."

And Pauline Kael, in *Kiss Kiss, Bang Bang,* wrote: "Whatever one thinks about it, it is a famous and impressive film. The performances by Montgomery Clift, Shelley Winters, and Elizabeth Taylor are good enough (and Clift is almost too good, too sensitive), though they appear to be over-directed pawns."

Variety: "For Miss Taylor, at least, the histrionics are of a quality so far beyond anything she has done previously that Stevens' skilled hands on the reins must be credited with a minor miracle."

"Miss Taylor deserves an Academy Award for her work," said *Boxoffice.* In the *New York Times,* A. H. Weiler, wrote: "Elizabeth Taylor's delineation of the rich and beauteous Angela is the top effort of her career. It is a shaded, tender performance and one in which her passionate and genuine romance avoids the pathos common to young love as it sometimes comes to the screen."

Howard Hughes was not the only man who admired Elizabeth Taylor at first from a distance and then used his wiles and his millions to move in closer. In fact, men were beginning to flock after Elizabeth Taylor like little beasties crawling out of the woodwork. But this one was no beastie. He was another prominent multimillionaire. Ironically, Glenn Davis proved to be the only man in Elizabeth Taylor's long list of fiancés who was *not* a millionaire.

This well-heeled suitor made his appearance while Elizabeth was working at Paramount. He took the shortest way to her door—a straight line. Through Pete Freeman, a friend whose father was a top executive at Paramount, he wangled an invitation to the set where Elizabeth and Clift were working. Pete and his wife accompanied the admirer to his quarry, and there let him fend for himself.

And so Elizabeth Taylor had lunch with Conrad Nicholson Hilton, II, the son of the multimillionaire hotel owner. Hilton was twenty-two at the time, a young man who had everything and had been everywhere (almost).

From the age of fourteen, he had spent his summers working his father's hotels. Then he had served a hitch in the Navy, had studied hotel management in Switzerland, and had become vice president and manager of the Bel-Air Hotel—not in the Hilton chain. He played the role of a bored and sophisticated playboy, and the role was not far from the truth.

Elizabeth was far from entranced. When her mother asked her if she had a nice time at lunch, Elizabeth sighed. "I guess so."

Hilton—called "Nicky" to his father's "Connie" —called the next day, and so Elizabeth invited him to dinner at the Taylors'.

"We liked him very much," Sara wrote later. Nicky was no fool. He invited the Taylors over to his father Connie's enormous mansion in Bel Air— a 64-room palace inside a landscaped estate. The Hiltons—Connie; Barron, Nicky's brother; and Marilyn, his sister-in-law—were suitably impressed by the Taylors.

All during this period of the mating rite, Nicky was on his best behavior. Since Elizabeth didn't smoke nor drink—part of her Christian Science upbringing—Nicky gave up both vices. Elizabeth began to thaw out a little. She seemed almost to enjoy being with him.

Now occurred one of those coincidences that are impossible to appreciate in a piece of fiction or in a motion picture, but which happen in real life so often that they are accepted as part of the warp and woof of life. Elizabeth's next motion picture was *Father of the Bride*. She was cast as the bride—at a time when her own role in real life was about to be the same. But no one knew that at the time.

The picture is a remarkably amusing treatment of the Great American Ritual, originally published as a novel by Edward Streeter. With Spencer Tracy cast as Father and Joan Bennett as Mother, ably supported by Billie Burke, Leo G. Carroll, Don Taylor and others, the film is a romp. It is one of Vincente Minnelli's best comedies.

Tracy steals the picture, but Elizabeth is able to hold her own even with the great old professional. The studio knew it had a winner even before the big bombshell burst and threw them into ecstasies.

The bombshell, of course, was Elizabeth's announcement that she would be playing the role of bride in her own real life. It all happened at her eighteenth birthday party. Nicky proposed to her again, and this time she accepted him. She told her parents that she didn't want to wait. She wanted to be married right away.

The marriage was set for May 6.

And M.G.M. went bananas. The release date for

the picture was set several weeks after the real wedding. How could public relations have done it any better?

But there were complications of one sort or another that almost threw the entire wedding out the window—similar to one crucial episode in the script. Elizabeth had not been paying too much attention to her fiancé's religion. He was Catholic. Elizabeth was a Protestant. And now, days before the wedding, Elizabeth received a real shock.

To marry him, she would have to swear an oath that she was eager for motherhood and would bring up her children as Catholic. She did not want to bring up her children as Catholic. This seemed to her to be an unreasonable request. For awhile she mulled over the idea of breaking off the engagement.

But the pressure was on, and she reluctantly agreed. It was not a good way to start a marriage. Elizabeth blamed herself for being naive, overprotected, and unworldly. She was right. She was usually a shrewd observer of character; but she was very unseeing when she looked at the men in her life. Although she had been dating Nicky for months, she did not perceive that he was a troubled young man. Nor did she learn from any of his friends that he had a nasty temper, that he had a compulsion to gamble, and that he was close to being a drug addict.

She liked his Texan drawl, and his way with her. He was the fun person she had always dreamed of.

In May, two months after her eighteenth birthday, M.G.M. masterminded a gigantic wedding that drew more press attention than anything in

Elizabeth's life to date. The ceremony was held at the Church of the Good Shepherd on Santa Monica Boulevard in Beverly Hills. Elizabeth's wedding dress was designed by the studio's Helen Rose.

The bridesmaids were Barbara Thompson, who had married Marshall Thompson, Elizabeth's first real date; Jane Powell, who had just married; and Betty Sullivan. There were photographers crawling all over the place. Twenty-five policemen tried to keep back 2,500 screaming-mad, half-hysterical, perspiring fans.

A fleet of M.G. limousines drove Elizabeth and the members of the bridal party to the church. Elizabeth was too swept up in the excitement to notice three telltale monitory signs:

As she got out of the limousine, her gown caught on the rear door.

When the procession started down the aisle, the organ suddenly ceased to function.

For some reason the Roman Catholic ceremony was five minutes late in starting.

But then, perhaps, these were simply accidents that meant nothing.

Elizabeth was not too alert that day, anyway. She had a bad cold, and had dosed herself with penicillin so she could struggle through the ceremony. It was a double-ring ceremony, presided over by Patrick J. Cancannon.

Afterward there was a double honeymoon—first a week in Carmel by the Sea and then several months in Europe.

While the Hiltons were in Europe, M.G.M. released *Father of the Bride*. It was a smash success.

"*Father of the Bride* is a honey of a picture of American family life," said Bosley Crowther, in the *New York Times*. And her real-life role was not overlooked by *Variety*, reporting on the "timely casting of Elizabeth Taylor as the bride (a role she just assumed in real life) to help stir wicket interest."

"Miss Taylor demonstrates that she is still in the promising-young-actress stage of her career. For quite a time to come, she is likely to stir up more fuss off screen than on," noted Alton Cook of the *New York World-Telegram* with some prescience.

The marriage was not the smash the picture was, at least, not in that sense.

Trouble began almost immediately. Rumors started flying. Gossip columnists spread the word that Nicky was drinking. Others said that Nicky was gambling.

Elizabeth wrote one ebullient letter from Paris. But after that, Sara and Francis did not hear a word from her all during the honeymoon trip. "The honeymoon in Europe lasted two weeks," Elizabeth wrote. "I should say the marriage lasted for two weeks." The itinerary included France, England, Italy and Switzerland. During the two-month stay on the French Riviera rumors of quarrels and spats began to appear in the newspapers.

"The fights get nastier and nastier," wrote Louella Parsons. "Nicky left his bride alone night after night in favor of the gambling tables. This was a new and unbearable situation for Elizabeth. No man had ever ignored her before, chosen to be elsewhere when he could be at her side."

A young bride who had shared confidences with

Elizabeth on the *Queen Mary* saw her at a casino
one night on the Riviera. Hilton, she recalled, was
playing for what looked like high stakes at the
gaming tables. "After a moment, I saw Elizabeth
sitting nearby, watching. I was struck by how different she looked. She had been so happy on the
ship and now she just seemed melancholy."

Elizabeth, with nothing to do but wait for her
husband to come home, began to smoke simply to
keep herself busy, and almost immediately developed into a chain smoker.

"We were both much too young and immature,
and our European honeymoon lasted too long,"
Elizabeth later said. "We had no feeling of security
or settling down. Until I was married, I had never
before spent a night away from my mother."

The honeymoon was over, in more ways than
one, when Elizabeth and her husband arrived in
New York. Her parents met them. Sara was
shocked. Elizabeth had lost twenty pounds and
was almost down to skin and bone. Besides that,
she was tight-lipped and uncommunicative.

"When I married Nick," she said later, "I fell off
my pink cloud with a thud."

For two months the newlyweds put on a happy
front. Elizabeth made what she later called "feeble
attempts" to run a house. Most of the time Nicky
was out on the golf course or at his desk running
the hotel. Elizabeth was now at the studio making
a sequel to *Father of the Bride,* called *Father's Little
Dividend.*

They began quarreling about everything. They
even quarreled about money—an unheard of thing
for a Hilton. Elizabeth resented the fact that even

though Nicky was her husband, he would not help pay for her lunches and her clothes. She even helped with a share of the expense of the house. Nicky paid the maid. Elizabeth bought the pots, pans and linens.

But she did not run home to her mother. Sara was bewildered. She wanted to be a confidante, but could not be if Elizabeth did not come to her.

Meanwhile the situation was becoming intolerable. Nicky's temper tantrums frightened Elizabeth. She finally moved out. But she didn't go home. Instead, she moved in with her M.G.M. stand-in, Margery Dillon.

Then, after a few nights, she stayed with Helen Rose, and then at the home of her agent, Jules Goldstone, and his wife. She even went home one night, but found she could not stay with her parents, who were far too overprotective.

She was a guest at the Goldstone home when Nicky finally located her and did everything he could to win her back. He sent her two dozen roses every day for a week, and kept calling her up to talk. He seemed almost recklessly determined to put the marriage back together again. Then, finally, Elizabeth decided that she had to divorce him.

She called him over to tell him. The two were closeted together for almost an hour. The Goldstones could hear Nicky's voice, suddenly rising in an almost banshee wail, and then four letter words of all kinds. The shouting became so loud that Goldstone finally went in and threw Nicky out of the house.

It was all over. Elizabeth was eighteen. The studio—her true surrogate father—managed her divorce almost as efficiently and smoothly as it had managed her wedding.

It was Elizabeth who wanted out. Nicky still wanted to keep going. In one outburst to the press, he tried to explain what came between them:

"It was life in a goldfish bowl. One time a battery of reporters and photographers invaded our suite—it happened all the time—and one of the photographers said to me, 'Hey, Mac, get out of the way, I want to snap a picture!'"

Nicky Hilton did not live a charmed life. Only seventeen years later, at the age of forty-two, he died of a heart attack.

"We were much too young," Elizabeth said then. "I'm sorry I hurt him."

The divorce decree was granted February 1, 1952, on the grounds of mental cruelty. No alimony was granted; none was asked.

"I've the body of a woman and the emotions of a child," said Elizabeth in trying to make some sense out of her shattered personal affairs.

CHAPTER FIVE
Double Bill

For Elizabeth Taylor the breakup of her marriage to Nicky Hilton was even more of a blow than it might have been to another person. Although she was eighteen years old, and looked older than she was, she had lived the life of a kind of fairy-tale princess. From the moment she awoke in the morning to the moment she went to bed at night she was programmed by her mother and her father (the M.G.M. one).

The words she spoke were words worked up by script writers; the emotions she displayed were those dreamed up by directors; the actions of her day were make-believe. She was a hollow person. That does not mean she was stupid; her very problem was her sharp intelligence. She *knew* she was living in an unreal world. She simply was unable to make contact with the real one.

The shattering realization that her marriage was doomed almost broke her down. She believed in marriage; she believed that her vows were forever, she wanted to be a housewife first and a career girl second. It was an impossibility. No one was to blame, although the sheltering she had experienced from her mother seemed to come to be the real villain.

Her guilt at the failure of her marriage, even though it was not totally her fault, prevented her from seeking solace and advice from her mother. She was ashamed; she turned in every direction but where she might have been helped.

"You try to make yourself believe everything is still beautiful," she said, referring to her groping after the breakup. "I worked very hard at this—perhaps too hard. My career gave me something to do."

More than that, her career gave her another person to cling to. He was a young director in his late twenties named Stanley Donen, in charge of the picture she was then making: ironically titled *Love Is Better Than Ever*. She was with him professionally most of the day, and their professional relationship shifted gears into a personal one.

Elizabeth Taylor was in miserable physical shape. She had no appetite. She came on the set white-faced, every nerve quivering, her body thin and wasted. She would sit brooding by herself and then suddenly burst out into hysterical tears.

When that happened, Donen closed down the set and tried to comfort her.

His efforts succeeded to a degree. But Elizabeth was a special case. From her earliest days, she was a totally dependent person: dependent on her mother and father at first; then, as she entered the motion picture business, dependent more and more on her mother alone. When she made the break with her mother and married Nicky Hilton, she shifted her allegiance to him, totally.

That was the reason her discovery of his inability to lead her was so totally shattering.

Now with her guilt preventing her from shifting her dependence back to her mother, she made the mistake of turning to a stranger—Stanley Donen. It was a mistake because it was a desperation move. Once she had turned to him, she couldn't let him go. She saw him every day for weeks and weeks, clinging to him more and more.

One of her most pressing problems at the time was a place to live. She did not want to go back home; that was out of the question. She discussed the problem with Jules Goldstone.

Goldstone suggested that she should hire a secretary-companion to live with. If she did so, he pointed out, she would stop any kind of negative gossip. And Goldstone knew a friend of his own secretary's, a young woman who had worked for Mrs. Bob Hope.

Elizabeth met Peggy Rutledge in Goldstone's office. Peggy was embarrassed, and so was Elizabeth. "I asked Elizabeth what we should talk about," she said. "[Elizabeth] said she hadn't the slightest idea. Then, I suddenly asked if I could make coffee; it turned out neither of us could cook."

Finally Peggy suggested that they try sharing an apartment. "If you don't like me, I'll leave. If I don't like you, I'll also leave."

Peggy went out and found two apartments. Elizabeth investigated the first and liked it. They moved into a five-room furnished apartment on Wilshire Boulevard in March 1951. Tony Curtis and Janet Leigh lived just downstairs.

Once the problem of where to live was solved, others cropped up. Neither of the two women could cook worth a damn. They were always burning the bottoms out of pots and spilling grease on the stove. Nor was housekeeping the forte of either.

And the studio was always on the phone with some complaint, minor or major. One major complaint that kept recurring was about Elizabeth's diction. "You've got to clean up her language!" one harried executive at Metro pleaded with Peggy. "Out of that beautiful face comes this *language*."

Peggy tried to put a stopper in Elizabeth's mouth, but she was unable to dry up the flow of blue invective. From the vantage point of 1981, four-letter words might seem to be a mild ailment in anyone's psyche, but M.G.M. was simon-pure about its "niceties." It considered itself the arbiter of all American mores. And Elizabeth's language was not that of Miss Nicey-Nicey 1951.

In fact, Elizabeth spent a good deal of her off-time with Montgomery Clift and Roddy McDowall, solid old friends through thick and thin. They were excellent therapy for her—good raconteurs, good actors, and good friends. Elizabeth once said that they both made her "feel loved," and at the same time they "weren't always trying to get serious."

Another more persistent problem continued to pertrub the M.G.M. front office. Elizabeth's health was definitely deteriorating. Although she had a friend in Stanley Donen, she loathed the picture she was working on. She had a right to. It was a lightweight romantic comedy about a dancer in love with a big-time talent scout. She was cast opposite Larry Parks. Parks was blacklisted for alleged Communist leanings during the shooting and the finished film was shelved for a time.

Prior to that role, Elizabeth had played a cameo bit—as herself—in *Callaway Went Thataway*, a comedy about the sagging career of a cowboy star and the attempts of a team of promoters to resurrect it.

Neither of these parts was enough to bolster her flagging morale. She felt her career was in jeopardy as well as her personal life. Brooding about the two upset her physiological balance. She wound up with a severe case of colitis. The studio doctors advised her to eat nothing but baby food.

"I grew thinner and thinner," she said. Panicked because even her own body was betraying her, Elizabeth clung to Donen more tightly. The studio began to fret about her emotional life. Sara herself took a dim view of Donen. When Elizabeth steeled herself enough to bring Donen home to meet the family, Sara picked a fight with her daughter. The two of them squared off in an old-fashioned brouha-ha right at the front door. Donen was forced to drive a shaken Elizabeth home to her apartment.

M.G.M. was worried. "A number of us thought that Donen was a fine guy, but not for Elizabeth," said one on the scene. "Finally we agreed that the best way to separate them was to send her abroad to make a picture."

And that led to another turning point in Elizabeth's life.

The picture the studio chose for this little ploy

was *Ivanhoe,* starring Robert Taylor and Joan Fontaine—Taylor as Ivanhoe, and Fontaine as Rowena. Elizabeth was cast as Rebecca, the Jewess. Although she may have suspected she was being maneuvered—later she called the picture "a piece of cachou" (a sweet pill)—she did little about it. Instead, she packed up her boxes of baby food, clothes, and left for London with her new companion, Peggy Rutledge.

She was in bad physical and emotional condition when she arrived. Her director, Richard Thorpe, was depressed when he saw her. "Then and later, I expected her to break down any minute."

These expectations did not prove out.

Elizabeth Taylor was never to be without the help of a man to set her aright, no matter what crisis she faced. The day after her arrival in London, pictures appeared in the newspapers showing her and Michael Wilding together again. Wilding had seen her during a short stay in Hollywood earlier in the year while making a movie.

"Stanley Donen was then the love of her life," he said. "I telephoned her in London to ask her out because I honestly thought she might be lonely. With Peggy Rutledge, we went to dinner that night and for the next five."

Somewhere along the line Peggy vanished from sight.

Wilding was a far better diet for her than baby food. He was a successful British actor who had won a poll as England's most popular male star two years before. Six feet tall, always dressed well, he was an amusing conversationalist. Twenty years Elizabeth's senior, Michael Charles Gauntlet Wilding, the son of a British Army captain, traced his family back to the Archbishop of Canterbury who crowned Queen Victoria and to John of Gaunt— "on the wrong side of the blanket."

Wilding was a graduate of Christ College (Oxford) and made his stage debut on the West End in 1939. He then made several movies and played in one of Alfred Hitchcock's all-time lows, *Under Capricorn,* opposite Ingrid Bergman. In spite of all that, he was called "England's Cary Grant."

Wilding was a genial, easygoing man. "At the sight of him, I decided to forget my baby food," said Elizabeth. "I ate anything I liked, and in a month, I was cured of all my ailments. And I finally proposed to him."

Wilding did not accept right away.

"We'd already said we loved each other, earlier," Elizabeth went on. "But he said I was too young, I'd change my mind. When I objected, he said we should wait."

They did. Actually, it was impossible for them to be married at the time, even if both had wanted to. Elizabeth's divorce would not become final until the following January. Wilding himself was married to actress Kay Young, and although separated from her for four years, he was still technically married.

Before she left London, Elizabeth wired her mother. It was the first time Sara had heard from her for many months.

WE ARE ALL THINKING OF YOU AND WISHING YOU WERE HERE. WE ARE HAVING A WONDERFUL REUNION TOGETHER. ALL VERY HAPPY. CAN'T

WAIT TO SEE YOU IN BEVERLY HILLS.
ALL OUR LOVE, ELIZABETH MELVINA
AND KENNY MCELDOWNEY AND
MICHAEL WILDING.

Sara remembered Michael Wilding. The others
were friends of hers. She had once thought that
Elizabeth was fascinated with Wilding. When she
met Elizabeth in New York shortly after her return
to the States, she was pleasantly surprised at the
change in her daughter. "She had gained back part
of her lost weight and the color in her cheeks. She
was looking radiantly happy."

Elizabeth stayed in New York for a while, tele-
phoning Wilding in England every day. Then she
left to celebrate her parents' twenty-fifth wedding
anniversary in Miami with Uncle Howard. In November, she was in New York again, this time
staying at the Plaza Hotel. When she arrived, the
management asked her how long she intended to
stay, and she told them five days.

They showed her an enormous suite, but in view
of the expense she asked for another. The management said the suite was on the house. She
moved in, delighted with the posh quarters. Instead
of five days, she stayed weeks.

Then M.G.M. finally asked her home for retakes
on *Ivanhoe*. When she checked out of the hotel she
was stunned to find that the management had
billed her for $2,500. Then it turned out that the
hotel had given her five days free, and charged her
for all the rest.

Through the red mist rising in front of her eyes,
Elizabeth imagined the fine hand of Conrad
Hilton, her ex-father-in-law, who owned the hotel.

She also saw that she had been taken, and taken very cleanly. One of her rages began to develop, and she called Montgomery Clift to tell him what had happened.

He too was outraged, and came over, bringing Roddy McDowall. One version of the story included even Merv Griffin, then an actor. He too was a close friend of both McDowall and Clift.

They ordered a bowl of martinis from room service and contemplated the problem as they finished off the martinis. Revenge was the order of the day. The group began taking pictures off the walls and hanging them upside down in different spots. They screwed out some of the bathroom fixtures, including the shower nozzle, and managed a large number of other depredations, including the staging of a tremendous flower fight in which stems, petals, and leaves of six dozen double chrysanthemums were strewed over all the rooms of the suite.

Clift lifted all the towels in the bathroom and packed them in Elizabeth's luggage. It was the kind of activity more indicative of the 1960s than of the 1950s. The upshot of it was that Elizabeth did pay the bill, but had her vengeance, too—although she called to apologize later for what she had done.

Once back in Hollywood, Elizabeth waited for Wilding to appear. He was in town to promote *Lady with a Lamp,* a picture he had made with Anna Neagle, in which she played Florence Nightingale. During his stay in Hollywood, he and Elizabeth were frequently in the company of Stewart Granger and his wife Jean Simmons.

Wilding had not yet made up his mind. Actually,

he was still involved deeply with Marlene Dietrich, although Elizabeth was not aware of this. The Dietrich-Wilding affair was at a dead end. Sheilah Graham noted that "Wilding was mad for her, and completely devoted to her, but she was not the marrying kind."

He had not lived with his wife since 1945. But he was still hesitant about making the break. One night when he was with Elizabeth he said, "Darling, you should wear sapphires to match your eyes."

Elizabeth seized the opportunity to ask his help in choosing between several sapphire rings she was thinking about buying. When the choice was made, she asked him to slip the ring onto the third finger of her left hand. And so it was decided.

Now Hedda Hopper got into the act—or at least that is the story she told in *All The Truth and Nothing But.* Many in Hollywood, she said, thought Wilding was not the man for her. "He's too sophisticated, too British, too old," friends said.

Hopper was even more specific. Inviting Wilding and Elizabeth to her place, she gave them a little lecture, intimating broadly that Wilding had no right to marry Elizabeth since his heart was already given to another—in this case, Stewart Granger!

"Are you going to marry a man like *that?*" she asked.

"I love him," Elizabeth said, and that was all.

Later, when the Hopper book was published in 1962, Wilding was long divorced from Elizabeth, but he sued Hopper for a bundle of money— $3,000,000—plus a public apology. Hopper had to settle out of court for a six-figure sum, and excise the offending material from the book.

In 1981, long after the Hopper book was published, a Stewart Granger biography included a section on the incident. Granger and Wilding had been friends since their early days in motion pictures. Granger said it was probably the most ridiculous idiocy in the world for Hopper to assume that Wilding—one of the "great cocksmen of all time"—was a homosexual.

Accordingly, when Wilding telephoned Granger after the scene in Hopper's house, Granger dialed Hopper and told her off in a short epithet including a four-letter Anglo-Saxon word beginning with "c" that quite probably curled her very proper hair.

But those revelations were far in the future.

Soon after Elizabeth's divorce became final in January 1952, she and Michael Wilding were married in a quiet ceremony in London's Caxton Hall registry office. It was February 21, 1952. Only fourteen people, including Wilding's parents, attended.

But the public was not far away. Television cameramen with telescopic lenses forted up in an office across the street and took news clips of the ceremony. In the streets a surging mob of 3,000 fans screamed and shoved to get a better view. In the battle to get through the hysterical mob, Elizabeth's hat was ripped from her head. She and Wilding were torn from each other by grabbing hands. A kind-hearted London bobby half-carried Elizabeth to the car.

There was a reception later at Claridge's, given by Herbert Wilcox, the producer husband of Wilding's co-star, Anna Neagle. Later a smaller gathering celebrated in the Wilding apartment. Late at night the bride and groom arrived at their suite in the Berkeley Hotel.

"For our wedding supper, we ordered pea soup, bacon and eggs, and champagne," Elizabeth recalled. "The waiter almost dropped dead."

Their wedding gifts were few in number, all from friends of Wilding: a crystal martini shaker, a pair of diamond earrings, and the *Oxford English Dictionary*.

They spent their eight-day honeymoon in the French Alps, and then returned to London to settle down in Wilding's London flat. There they stayed for some time.

Elizabeth had turned her back on Hollywood. "I had no acting ambition at all—I didn't even want to be an actress any more," she recalled. "All I wanted at first was to be Mike's wife and to have a baby right away. Where we were to live I left entirely up to him; while I like California better, I could live happily in London or Rome."

Wilding finally decided to move to California. He liked the informality of the States. Besides that, he had just signed a three-year contract with M.G.M.

Meanwhile, Elizabeth's seven-year contract was just running out. Now came a hard decision for her to make. Should she re-sign? There were things she loathed about M.G.M. Hollywood was changing. Some newcomers to the business were making more money acting as free-lances rather than as contract players.

It was money which finally forced her to make a decision. Money and a little luck.

The picture she was scheduled to make was

called *The Girl Who Had Everything*. She started work in the spring of 1952. Wilding finished the picture he was making in London and flew out to the Coast where he began looking all over town for a house. And finally he found one he liked.

The woman who had everything in the picture did indeed have everything in real life. In June Elizabeth discovered that she was pregnant. Now it was necessary to have a place to bring up the baby. Wilding finally found a two-bedroom cottage on a large acre-and-three-quarter lot on the top of a hill. The living quarters were spacious, but broken up into separate areas resembling rooms.

Outside there was a separate guest house attached by a porte-cochere. That cottage contained a bedroom, living room, kitchen and bath. And there was plenty of room for the pets that Elizabeth would have. House and cottage needed some remodeling, and while this would add on another $50,000 to the initial cost of $75,000, the place looked like a good buy for what they needed.

They bought it. And those two facts—the fact that she was pregnant, and the fact that the house was past their means—forced her to sign with M.G.M. for the second time. There were also more human and personal reasons. "I re-signed because I got cornball-sentimental about Benny Thau and all the other nice people at the studio, and because I thought Michael and I would both be working there and we could have lunch together.

"But, mainly, it was because I was pregnant. We needed money to get a home of our own—a nest in which to hatch the eggs."

Her salary was $4,750 a week at the time. $247,000 a year? Figure it out. But, no. No way.

Really only $190,000. Oh, plenty of money, sure.
But the studios were always clever at squeezing
blood out of a turnip: their "year" figured to only
40 weeks!

She signed without informing the studio that she
was pregnant. Then, once M.G.M. finished *The
Girl Who Had Everything,* she told them. The brass
immediately slapped a suspension on her. Apparently pregnancy was something not quite con-
doned in the real world, only in Mayer's make-believe world of celluloid. When she was through
playing around at being a mother, she could come
back to work at her regular salary.

This was a nasty blow to the strapped Wildings.
They were forced to borrow a large amount of
money from M.G.M., advances on Wilding's
salary for the three pictures he was signed for, and
on Elizabeth's salary when she got back to
work.

"Every time I got pregnant," she remarked,
"kind-hearted old M.G.M. would put me on suspension."

The baby wasn't due until January 16, 1953, but
he was born on January 6, by Caesarean section.
An examination had showed that she would have
to be operated on immediately. She was rushed to
Santa Monica Hospital. Fans appeared from out
of the blue, swarming about in the corridors.

"Michael, Michael, Michael!" she called as she
was being wheeled down one of the halls. He ran
after her to try to be beside her when she went back
to her room. Fans rushed after him and stood outside the door while she tried to get some rest.

Michael Howard Wilding Jr. weighed 7 pounds
and 5 ounces at birth.

Elizabeth turned down the studio some weeks later when they offered her a clinker called *All the Brothers Were Valiant*. Next she found she was on loan to Paramount Pictures to replace Vivien Leigh in *Elephant Walk*. Leigh was suffering from an acute nervous breakdown. It was a kind of an Indian *Rebecca/Cimarron/Dragonwyck/Under Capricorn*—the creaky old plot about the bride struggling against an alien tradition that almost overwhelms her.

On the last day of shooting, the "accident" tradition exerted itself on Elizabeth. She was posing for stills when a wind machine hurled a fragment of steel into her eye. For three days she walked around with a sore eye; an eye doctor finally removed the steel splinter but found that her eye had ulcerated. She lay in bed with both eyes bandaged for days—close to losing the sight of the eye.

Although it resembled a kind of sick joke, Teitelbaum, a famed Hollywood furrier, sent her an ermine eye patch during her convalescence. "How I loved the idea!" said Elizabeth. The eye healed. She did not lose it.

By now it was becoming apparent that Elizabeth was accident prone. "If she opens a beer can, she cuts herself; if there is a chair in the middle of the set, she falls over it while talking over her shoulder to someone," said Richard Brooks, one of her directors.

M.G.M. had its revenge on Elizabeth for her motherhood. They put her into two real ciphers one right after the other:

Rhapsody started out as a novel called *Maurice Guest,* written by an Austrian woman named Henry Handel Richardson. At the time it was written in

1908 it was a perceptive study of a music student and of an unhappy love affair that leads to his suicide.

Changes were instituted. Instead of Germany, it took place in Switzerland. Instead of focusing on the music student, it focused on his girl friend. And the crucial plot twist, his suicide, was softened to temporary alcoholism.

With these handicaps, Elizabeth performed as well as she could. "Under these difficult cirumstances, without flair in either script or direction, even her evident and genuine beauty seems at times to be a fake," said Otis L. Guernsey, Jr., in the *New York Herald Tribune*.

"The picture will not find the boxoffice-going easy," said *Variety,* calling it a "pot-boiler" of a plot stretched over "an unnecessarily long one hour and 55 minutes." Bosley Crowther, of the *New York Times,* wrote: "Miss Taylor never looked lovelier. . . . Any gent who would go for music with this radiant—and rich—Miss Taylor at hand is not a red-blooded American. Or else he's soft in the head."

Next came *Beau Brummel,* with Stewart Granger, Peter Ustinov, and Robert Morley. It was a remake of the ancient Clyde Fitch play. Elizabeth had to wear a blond wig. There was nothing in the role to get her teeth into.

"As for Miss Taylor, she is decorative, but something less than useful as a heroine who cannot quite make up her mind between Beau and a stolid young lord," wrote Otis L. Guernsey, Jr., of the *New York Herald Tribune*.

Monthly Film Bulletin took aim at her: "Elizabeth Taylor makes a barely articulate Lady Patricia." The *New Yorker* through John McCarten complained that Lady Patricia, "as enacted by Elizabeth Taylor, is a misty, if beautiful type." Whatever that meant.

Next came *The Last Time I Saw Paris,* an update of the old F. Scott Fitzgerald short story, "Babylon Revisited." In this one Elizabeth played opposite Van Johnson, with Walter Pidgeon, Donna Reed, Roger Moore, and Eva Gabor in the cast.

It was far from a great picture, but Elizabeth Taylor did well in it. The story is about a reformed drunk who tries to reclaim custody of his daughter from a hateful sister-in-law. In the long flashback detailing the sot's earlier progress, Elizabeth played opposite Johnson with authority.

The critics bought it. "Performancewise, Miss Taylor's work as the heroine should be a milestone for her," said *Variety.* "It is her best work to date and shows a thorough grasp of the character, which she makes warm and real, not just beautiful."

Film Daily called it "the best performance of her career." The *New York Herald Tribune* paid particular attention to Johnson's role as well as Elizabeth's. "She is not only a stunning creature but a vibrant one as she flings herself into the role of an impetuous, alluring, pleasure-loving beauty."

Elizabeth became pregnant again. This time she was reluctant to tell the studio, knowing that she would be put on immediate suspension. Meanwhile, the Wildings had outgrown the tiny house they lived in, and had located an eight-room place with a swimming pool on Summit Drive. Its cost was $150,000; they wanted to buy it.

It was a big glass-and-adobe place, in modern design. With so many windows, it seemed to be outdoors as much as indoors. On an end wall finished in bark, clumps of ferns grew. A garden inside contains a driftwood tree that appeared to support the ceiling. There was a chimneyless fireplace in a 45-foot fieldstone wall along one side of the living room. From one glass wall the swimming pool could be viewed from inside.

She couldn't afford to go on suspension again, but she was going to be out for a while. She made a deal with them; she added one year onto her seven-year contract. It was to prove a major obstacle in the future—although she had no idea of it at the time.

Wilding was thinking that Elizabeth should buy out of her contract and free lance. "With luck," he said, "she can earn one million dollars in seven years and be independent the rest of her life." This was possibly the understatement of the decade, but neither of the Wildings knew it at the time. It was hard enough getting the $150,000 to buy their new house. As it was, they had to come to terms with M.G.M. once again; the studio put up the money —for its pound of flesh.

Christopher Edmund Wilding was born on February 27, 1955, by Caesarean section. He weighed 5 pounds, 12 ounces at birth.

With the two children in the big comfortable house, it assumed a casual formality that sometimes resembled a zoo more than a house. There were three Siamese cats, four dogs, a batch of miniature French poodles and almost anything else that wandered in. It was such a warm kind of place to be no one really noticed that there were tiny chinks beginning to appear in the façade of the perfect marriage.

CHAPTER SIX
Shadow No More

To date the picture that had shown Elizabeth Taylor at her best as an emotional actress of stature was *A Place in the Sun.* She had learned a great deal from George Stevens, who had extracted exceptional performances from his three principals: Montgomery Clift, Shelley Winters, and Elizabeth.

Elizabeth had learned almost as much from watching Clift as she had from taking instruction from Stevens. She watched him as he drove himself into the role he was playing; she tried the same trick herself.

"Monty is the most emotional actor I have ever worked with," she said. "And it is contagious. When he would start to shake, I would start to shake."

Now George Stevens was trying to find an actress for the role of the spoiled daughter in *Giant,* which he was making for Warner Brothers from the Edna Ferber novel. He wanted Grace Kelly. She was cool and elegant and *looked* rich and spoiled. But she was unavailable. Stevens finally settled on Elizabeth Taylor. She earned no extra money for the job. She was paid only her regular M.G.M. salary. The studio made $150,000 by lending her out to Warner Brothers.

Elizabeth's work on *Giant* was complicated by the fact that the Wilding marriage was beginning to unravel in a way that was obvious even to acquaintances not close to the couple. The truth of the matter was that when Elizabeth married Wilding she was looking for a father; she had found Nicky Hilton a bad substitute and needed someone to lean on. Her own father was affectionate, but not demonstrative. In Elizabeth's world—that of make-believe—demonstration of affection was the name of the game.

Wilding's interests were quite different from Elizabeth's. "I believe she bored him," one acquaintance said. "I *know* he bored her."

Besides that, there were professional problems. Wilding's career, which had been moving along successfully in London, was beginning to flounder in Hollywood. He was cast against such formidably emasculating actresses as Joan Crawford, in *Torch Song*, in which he played a blind pianist whose job was mainly to make Crawford look good. Then he was loaned to Fox for *The Egyptian* in which he played a kind of forlorn Pharoah wandering about Egypt trying to sell his people on the idea of One God. Then he was cast as Prince Charming in *The Glass Slipper* opposite Leslie Caron, and then played a role in *The Scarlet Coat,* something murky about Benedict Arnold. And there was *Zarak Khan,* some kind of exotic mishmash.

Elizabeth made no attempt to play down the rumors of a rift between them. "We don't pick and quarrel, but we do fight—it's garbage to say we don't." And she went on: "I think it's healthy to blow your lid now and then. What infuriates me about Michael is that he can be so underplaying. My temper is Irish, and when I blow, I blow. But while I am shouting in an Irish temper, there is he, blasé and unruffled. Finally, I yell at him, 'Oh, you —you—you—*Englishman!*'"

Part of the problem stemmed from the typical enforced absence of each partner in pursuit of his or her cinema career.

"We don't mind," Elizabeth told a reporter. "If one of us is working in Hollywood, then we're together. If one is working abroad, the other goes over whenever possible."

When Wilding was making *Zarak Khan* in Spanish Morocco, Elizabeth joined him to stay for a month. But when Elizabeth made *Beau Brummel,* Wilding was unable to stay with her in England for income tax reasons. He lived in Paris and she flew over every weekend to be with him.

"It was boring for me in Paris," Wilding admitted. "I just drifted about all week." On the weekend, it wasn't so bad. One night started at 8 o'clock with champagne dinner at the Berkeley and wound up twelve hours later in a workers' restaurant with onion soup and red wine.

"It was the most wonderful night of my whole life," said Elizabeth.

Wilding found some minor frustrations. "The thing I find difficult is her lack of any sense of time —she was *born* without any sense of time." That was a sore spot with her. And it was a true problem. In her professional life she had missed as many planes as she had caught. She had mislaid her passport time after time. For years she never even owned a watch. She frequently kept over a hundred people waiting on the set while she looked for her missing bra.

She was a primper. Habitually she took two hours to dress. She was once asked what took her so long. "I tint my fingernails, then my toenails. I cut my hair. I pluck my eyebrows. I brush and rebrush my hair. Also, I do all my Walter Mittying when I'm making up—I sit with lipstick in hand reliving a scene that took place last week, wishing I'd said this instead of that."

But then, when she was through, she looked just like Elizabeth Taylor—and so who cared?

In addition to the fact that Wilding knew he was slipping as Elizabeth was gaining, there were other complications. Her health was still shaky, at best. During a tour the two took in Scandinavia after the operation to save her eye, she had simply collapsed from exhaustion. The emotional turmoil resulted from the pressure of her half-mad fans.

"We were pursued by crazy, film-struck fans wherever we went," Wilding said. "They even behaved like maniacs, storming over us like wolf packs for autographs, poking pens in our eyes, and tearing our clothes."

As Mrs. Wilding, Elizabeth was, unbelievably, the most reserved of guests at a party. She would sit quietly in the corner, while others were outperforming each other. "I used to watch, observe, overhear conversations, and make my own comments to myself, some cynical. I was never bored, but neither did I mix."

With Wilding, she seemed more like his daughter than his wife. "I'd follow him from group to group like a puppy dog." One night at a party at the Charles Vidors' she made a trip to the powder room and as she came out she ran into Humphrey Bogart.

"Where's Michael?" she asked in a wee supplicating voice.

Bogart stared at her, his stone face unmoving. He decided not to speak and started to move off. Then, at the last moment, he swung around and shook his head.

"Let me talk to you, kid," he said, like a line out of one of his pictures. "It's damned stupid for you to keep following your husband around. You should be asserting yourself. Be something in your own right. Stop being a goddamned shadow."

And she began to change. She realized she was too dependent on Wilding. And that brought about another change in her psyche. She began to challenge opinions of his that she had been afraid to judge before. Arguments about contracts, arguments about movies, arguments about their life together sometimes ended with her acrimonious challenge:

"I'm not your daughter. I'm your wife."

Wilding had to accept it. "I thought I'd influence this trembling little creature," he said, without irony. "I thought I'd guide her along life's stony path." It wasn't to be that way at all. "Lately, I'm simply told to shut up. Marriage is a loving work. But it's a work."

The unraveling seams were beginning to show

when Elizabeth went to Marfa, Texas, to work on location in *Giant*. Stevens proved to be an even tougher taskmaster this time than he had been when she worked with him on *A Place in the Sun*.

There were big arguments over costumes even before shooting started. Elizabeth rebelled at wearing thick brogue shoes, heavy stockings, a long skirt, and a man's slouch hat over her hair done up in a tight bun. It was supposed to make her look desperate and sad.

"I felt like a damned fool and worse," she complained. "I couldn't see why the girl, an utterly feminine woman, would deliberately put on a ludicrous getup that made her look like a Lesbian in drag."

The fight continued as the cameras were readied to shoot the scene. Stevens accused her of being concerned only with looking glamorous. In a rage, Elizabeth wiped all her makeup off, loosened her hair and yanked it back, twisted it into two strands and slipped a rubber band over it. No hat. And they did the scene.

Later on antagonism erupted once again between Stevens and Elizabeth. In a scene in which Elizabeth and Rock Hudson played the estranged husband and wife, the two of them were to look at one another while witnessing someone else's marriage. No words—just the look.

Rehearsals were over. The cast broke for lunch. Elizabeth's dress was to be pressed. She waited in her dressing room for the call. An hour later, no call. Seventy-five extras were out there.

"What the hell are they doing?" Elizabeth asked her makeup man and hairdresser. "My God, it's been hours."

Finally she went out onto the set. The lights were off. The extras were standing around.

"What's going on?" Elizabeth asked Stevens, who was slumped in his chair, his chin in his hand.

He looked up. "Who the hell do you think you are?"

"What?"

"We have been waiting here for over an hour. Just who the hell do you think you are to keep these people waiting?" He gestured to the extras, the crew, everyone around.

Elizabeth straightened. "I didn't know you were waiting for me. Why wasn't I called?"

"Don't give me that!" snapped Stevens. "Just how far do you think you can go? Just how much do you think you can get away with? What did you do when you came back from lunch?"

Elizabeth blinked. "Well, I had my lunch hour and I came back, I fixed my makeup, they ironed my dress and I've been waiting in the dressing room."

Stevens growled, "I suppose you think that your makeup is more important than those people's makeup. I suppose you think your costume is more important than *their* costumes. Well, I have news for you. It isn't."

Elizabeth was near tears. "That wasn't what I meant. I've been waiting in there. No one called me."

He stared at her.

She began weeping. "Oh, go to hell!" she snapped and went off the set. By the time she had questioned several of the assistant directors, she found that whoever had been delegated to call her to the set had not done so.

"George," the first assistant director told Stevens, "it turns out that no one delivered the message. The ball got fouled."

Stevens said nothing to her.

He ordered the scene to proceed. Elizabeth was quivering, still very weepy and upset. There was only one take.

"I've always wondered," Elizabeth wrote later, "whether he did all that deliberately for the sake of the scene."

Working on *Giant,* Elizabeth formed a strong attachment to James Dean. Dean made only a few pictures in Hollywood but he was a cult figure of tremendous strength. Some time before the revolt of the 1960s, Dean was exhibiting that same spirit of rebellion in his personality. He was somewhat like Montgomery Clift. He kept to himself, and did not participate in the usual hijinks around the set.

His was a kind of Method-type acting that was extremely personal and extremely sensitive. Because he kept to himself, Elizabeth found herself drawn to him. The two of them got along better together than with other members of the cast.

Dean's part in the picture was finished before Elizabeth's. Because of his mania for driving his car at the fastest possible speed, he had been restricted from driving during the filming of the picture because of insurance provisions. He had a kind of self-destructive urge that many youths had at the time. Now that his scenes were in the can, the restriction was lifted and he took off.

The film was in the process of being wrapped up at the studio in Hollywood when his Porsche was involved in a high-speed accident on Highway 99 and Dean was killed instantly. At the time it happened, Elizabeth and the cast were watching the day's rushes in the projection room at the studio.

Only an hour after he was found dead in the wreck, news came to the projection room. Stevens took the call, said, "No, my God! When? Are you sure?" And then he hung up. Finally when the rushes were over, he turned up the lights.

"I've just been given the news that Jimmy Dean has been killed." And he elaborated.

Within two hours, the news was confirmed. By nine o'clock the studio was deserted. Elizabeth started for her car in the parking lot and met Stevens, who was just getting into his Mercedes.

"I just can't believe it," Elizabeth said. "I can't believe it."

Stevens said, "I believe it. He had it coming to him. The way he drove, he had it coming."

She went home, stunned and upset. She was unable to sleep all night. In the morning she dragged herself out of bed. Wilding advised her to stay home. Stevens was shooting the last scenes of the movie. He insisted that everyone be on the set. Wilding argued with him, but Stevens was adamant.

Wilding drove Elizabeth to the studio where she arrived looking rebellious and half-sick. There was an upsetting argument between her and Stevens. It ended when she screamed at him that he was a heartless son of a bitch.

She then played a long, six-minute scene in which she was in the makeup of an old woman. She had to wear rubber bags under her eyes. The scene was shot over and over all through the day.

"She didn't play it very well," Stevens said. "It

was the final scene and I'd wanted to complete the picture. But I knew we'd have to do it over again."

But the next day Elizabeth was in the hospital, with what was diagnosed as a twisted colon.

"If I hadn't had that blow-up with George Stevens, hysterical and crying, and if I hadn't eaten, it wouldn't have happened," she said later. There was no operation. But she was forced to stay in the hospital for two weeks before she could return to the studio to make the last scene.

The entire company waited for her until that time.

Once the picture was over, she settled down to wait for her next assignment. That was *Raintree County,* an adaptation of a best-selling first novel by Ross Lockridge, who had killed himself shortly after the publication of the book. About that time *Confidential*—a scandal sheet aimed at Hollywood professionals—came out with a story titled "When Liz Taylor's Away, Mike Will Play." According to the magazine, Wilding and a friend had brought a couple of strippers up to the house for a poolside after-hours act one night when Elizabeth was on location in Marfa, Texas, in June.

A gossip columnist called Wilding to find out how Elizabeth had reacted to the story. He had not even heard about it. After rushing out to buy the magazine, he was aghast at it, and apologetic to Elizabeth. She read it and blanched. But she put the best interpretation on it:

"Whether it's true or not," she said, "you can't let an article like that break up your marriage."

It was a brave front. Inwardly Elizabeth was seething. She was in the position of looking like a fool in front of all her peers. *Confidential* was an earlier version of the *National Enquirer,* but to date, no one in Hollywood had taken the magazine on to cool the fervor of its itch for prurience.

By now the Wildings' friends included Montgomery Clift, who was scheduled to work with Elizabeth in *Raintree County;* Kevin McCarthy, one of Clift's best friends and a friend of Elizabeth's; Rock Hudson, whom Elizabeth had met and liked on the *Giant* set; and others. With the marriage between Wilding and Elizabeth definitely going to pieces, it helped to have people around.

Raintree County was a sprawling, incoherent story that spanned three generations—about a typical American hero and a wife plunging into madness. In the screen version the story never really gets off the ground. Yet Elizabeth was happy to be acting with Clift once again. They worked on their scenes together with the intensity they had developed during the filming of *A Place in the Sun.*

Clift was developing into a true alcoholic. He would frequently drink himself into total oblivion. And his driving was getting worse. He was not quite so suicidal about speed as James Dean had been, but he was a danger on the highway. His own life was giving him trouble; his career was moving ahead, but his personal relationships were murky and clouded. He had been picked up for soliciting a man on 42nd Street. Hedda Hopper had a story that Clift had been picked up in New Orleans for pederasty, but that story turned out to be a fake: he was simply picked up for drunkenness.

With his drinking, he was now mixing in pills of

all kinds. Although he seemed his usual self during
the filming of *Raintree County,* he was spending
more and more hours by himself away from people. Elizabeth invited him to the house time and
again, but Clift apparently was upset at being used
as a sounding board for the Wildings in their disintegrating marriage situation. First Wilding would
want Clift's sympathy and then Elizabeth would
cry on his shoulder. He was fed up.

However, on the night of May 12, 1956, he did
come up to the Wilding house on Summit Drive.
He knew enough about his condition to realize
driving was dangerous for him. He had hired a
chauffeur to take him to and from the studio. But
on that night he was tired and determined not to
drive anywhere; he had sent the chauffeur home
early. With Elizabeth's insistent calls, he got in the
car and drove over, although he had not been behind the wheel of any car for months.

Kevin McCarthy was present, along with Rock
Hudson and his secretary, Phyllis Gates. Clift was
morose and quiet during the meal, but that was not
unusual. Afterwards, he drank a little wine. Finally
he decided he had to leave. A heavy Southern California fog had come up outside, making visibility
unsafe for any kind of driving. McCarthy offered
to lead him down the hill to be sure he managed the
dangerous curves safely.

As they got into their cars, Clift and McCarthy
chatted a moment. Clift was depressed about *Raintree County*—he knew the film was a bomb, and
that nothing he could do about it would help. He
told McCarthy how much he hated working in
Hollywood. Then he got in his car.

McCarthy noticed that Clift's car was following too close to his and he wondered if Clift might not be trying to play a chicken game the way he used to —bumping McCarthy's car from the rear. He accelerated. Clift followed closely, skidding and careening through the twisting street behind him. Then McCarthy saw Clift's car weaving from side to side, out of control.

"I heard a terrible crash," McCarthy said. He screeched to a stop and ran back through the fog. Clift's car was crumpled against a telephone pole— totally demolished. He smelled raw gasoline and reached in to turn off the ignition. It was too dark to see Clift.

He drove back to Elizabeth's house in anguish, yelling at them to call an ambulance. He was white and shaken. "Monty's had an accident and I can't get him out of the car."

Elizabeth determined to go down to help with Clift. Wilding and McCarthy tried to stop her. "She fought us off like a tiger, and raced down the hill," McCarthy said.

The group drove down to the wreck. Elizabeth climbed out and saw Clift. "His face was gushing blood," she said. "I couldn't see Monty at all. But I crawled into the car and put his head in my lap. Finally he came to, and he began to try to pull out a loose tooth. He asked me to pull out that one and another, and I did. I had to use control not to get sick. You could hardly see his face. It was like pulp. He was suffering from shock, but he was absolutely lucid."

They waited forty-five minutes for the ambulance. It got lost. Reporters and photographers

appeared long before the ambulance, all eager for
pictures of the injured actor. Hudson, McCarthy,
and Wilding, expensive motion picture talent all,
blockaded the wreck where Elizabeth sat with
Clift's head in her lap.

"Take us," they said, baring their teeth in
ghoulish grins.

Elizabeth drove to Cedars of Lebanon Hospital
with him. By the time they reached the hospital, his
head was horribly swollen. "His eyes by then had
disappeared," Elizabeth said. "His cheeks were
level with his nose. The whole head was like a giant
red soccer ball."

At Cedars of Lebanon the damage was assessed:
lacerations on the left side of his face; a broken
nose and crushed sinus cavity; both sides of the jaw
broken; two front teeth lost; severe cerebral con-
cussion; and whiplash.

He recovered—but he was never really the same
man ever again.

After six weeks of recuperation, the picture continued. Although both Clift and Elizabeth got
good reports from the critics, the picture did not
make money. It was too cumbersome, too mixed-
up.

Shortly before Clift was out of the hospital and
back on the set, McCarthy visited the Wildings
with his wife. He had tickets for a yacht ride. Mc-
Carthy was working as an assistant director for a
producer named Michael Todd. Todd was shooting part of an epic he was making called *Around the
World in 80 Days*—the old Jules Verne thriller up-
dated. McCarthy was working on the sequence of
the burning boat, to be shot near Santa Monica.

After shooting, the yacht was sailing on to Santa Barbara. Todd had been sending out invitations to Hollywood people through his actors and assistants. Did the Wildings want to come along?

Elizabeth had never been quite so down. Her marriage was almost over. Her picture career was ebbing. Her best friend was in the hospital with a ruined face. She needed some fun. She and her husband decided to take up McCarthy's offer.

They went on the yacht trip.

It was the end of the Wilding marriage, if it had not really ended long before.

It was also the beginning of another life for Elizabeth Taylor.

CHAPTER SEVEN
Around Michael Todd for 384 Days

Mike Todd was born Avrom Hirsch Goldbogen in Minneapolis on June 22, 1909, although in his later years Todd claimed he could not remember the date at all. He was the son of a rabbi. His mother wanted him to settle down and be a rabbi too, but Goldbogen had no intention of doing so. He was essentially a talker and a seller—of newspapers, of shoe shines, of vegetables, and eventually of real estate, of talent, and of hit shows like *Mexican Hayride, Star and Garter, The Hot Mikado,* and others.

He had a glib tongue, an ability to turn on the charm, and ambition that was a yard wide and a mile long. Whenever a carnival came to Minneapolis, he would get some kind of job and study all the people there. He loved show business.

But it wasn't at show business that he made his first million. By the time was was nineteen, he had made a fortune in real estate. Almost immediately he lost it. Chicago was an exciting place, but Goldbogen decided he wanted to try out his wings on the West Coast.

By now he had reasoned that the name he had
been born with was more a burden than an asset.
When he was very young he had had difficulty
speaking the word for "coat"—he called it a
"toat." His seven brothers and sisters called him
that—it was his family nickname.

So now he called himself "Todd," a kind of
bastardization of "Toat." He picked up the name
Michael because he liked the sound of it. He was
Michael Todd when he reached Hollywood.

Sound had just been added to the movies when
he got there. He knew there was a fortune to be
made in it, but he wasn't a technician. However, he
was an excellent entrepreneur. So he became a
building contractor, making another million building sound stages for the studios.

And he lost that million, too.

"I've never been poor," Todd once said, "only
broke. Being poor is a frame of mind. Being broke
is only a temporary situation."

By 1933 he was back in Chicago again, this time
in the middle of the World's Fair. His old carny
instincts surfaced once again, and he produced an
act called "The Flame Dance." This one involved a
girl dressed like a moth who danced around a huge
candle until her costume appeared to burn off,
leaving her in her birthday suit. Todd used a blow
torch to singe off the dancer's outer layer, leaving
her with only an inner layer to cover her—a kind of
flesh-colored leotard. "I burned up four girls per-
fecting that act," Todd once said.

Next he tried Broadway. His first two attempts
were giant flops. But the third was *The Hot
Mikado,* starring Bill Robinson. Essentially it was

the old Gilbert and Sullivan operetta—performed by blacks, in swing time.

More hits: *Star and Garter,* with Gypsy Rose Lee, and *Something for the Boys* with Ethel Merman.

"Dames and comedy," Todd once said. "I believe in giving the customers a meat and potatoes show. High dames and low comedy. That's my message."

Within a few years he was bankrupt again. In court he testified that he had gambled away maybe a quarter of a million dollars. But then he was back again with another idea. This one was called "Cinerama," and he became a partner with a group that put the widescreen effort over.

Todd thought Cinerama could be improved. Todd-AO was his version of Cinerama. This was the widescreen operation filmed with one lens rather than Cinerama's three.

Todd, one of the most persuasive talkers in the world, could con anyone. One moment he might be putting the convincer on Noel Coward to star in a show, the next he might be chewing out a worker for doing a sloppy job for him with four letter words that would singe a dockwalloper's hair.

He had so much energy he *exuded* it. Elizabeth Taylor recalled once that before she met him she had sat near his swimming pool on a rubber divan that had seats on both sides. "Our backs were about three inches apart," she said. "I remember that gave me a weird but overpowering feeling. It was as though my spine were tingling. I finally got up and moved."

It turned out that Todd was having the same feelings about Elizabeth.

More than that, she simply recalled seeing pictures of him sitting in the middle of a lot of half-dressed girls with a huge cigar in his mouth. To her, he was "extremely vulgar."

He was ostentatious about his possessions. One of the first bigshots to have a telephone in his limousine, he delighted in opening his window at a stop light and handing the telephone out to the driver of the car beside him: "It's for you."

He was once talking on his limo phone to a man he didn't particularly like and broke in to tell him, "Sorry, but I'm wanted on the other phone."

He signed a photograph of himself and gave it to his then press agent. "You made me what I am today," he had written, "but I still like you."

In the 1950s Todd was onto another big project. It was a film of the Jules Verne fun-classic, *Around the World in 80 Days*. And it was to be made in his new process, Todd-AO. The "AO" stood for American Optical, the company that had developed the process for him.

Oklahoma! was filmed in 1955 in Todd-AO, and by that time, history had repeated itself, and Mike Todd was no longer in charge of Todd-AO but had been pushed out of it. He needed to recoup. He went to his strength then, not to his weakness. His weakness, according to biographer Art Cohn, was that he was "only half-smart when it came to finances." He could make it, but it always disappeared. His strength was show business.

Todd had bought the screen rights to the Verne story and he knew the ingredients were right for a widescreen spectacle. He loved what he called "cameo" shots—short takes with famed actors and actresses. In *Around the World* he had Marlene Dietrich, an old flame of Todd's—ironically recalling the fact that Michael Wilding was also an old flame of Dietrich's—John Gielgud, Charles Boyer, Noel Coward, and Frank Sinatra.

Not everybody loved Mike Todd. S. J. Perelman, who wrote the script to *Around the World,* called his salary a "pittance . . . extracted only by deep surgery." He got $29,000, less 10 percent for his agent. "Our impresario," he wrote, "lived like the Medici, running up awesome bills that he waved away airily on presentation." The finances of the picture he said, were as "impenetrable as the Mato Grosso."

Todd was living with Evelyn Keyes at the time he first met Elizabeth Taylor. She had played Suellen, Scarlett O'Hara's sister in *Gone With the Wind.* She had also been married to Charles Vidor, John Huston, and Artie Shaw.

Todd could con his women as well as his men. When he met Elizabeth Taylor and found her desirable, he also found that a vacuum existed in the relationship between Elizabeth and her husband.

"We were then living as brother and sister," Elizabeth later confirmed.

Evelyn Keyes soon found herself dispatched to remote areas of the world to help promote the coming of *Around the World.* Because special equipment had to be provided for the showing of the picture, Todd *had* to do the thing as a program show at each site. Exit Evelyn Keyes.

The splitup between Elizabeth and Michael

Wilding was handled with the precision of a fine surgeon. Again the studio made the quiet announcement of their separation on July 19, 1956.

"Much careful thought has been given to the step we are taking," the statement read, showing that the statement as well as the step had been mulled over by more heads than one, although not one of the many high-level heads had thought to edit out the split infinitive that followed: "It is being done so that we will have an opportunity to thoroughly work out our personal situation. We are in complete accord in making this amicable decision."

One day later—June 20—Elizabeth had a phone call. It was Todd.

"I have to see you right away." Although she was a bit put out at being ordered around rather than *asked,* a mystified Elizabeth promised to meet him at the studio.

When Elizabeth arrived at M.G.M., she found that although she was on time—which in itself tended to be an unusual situation—Todd was late. She wandered into Benny Thau's office with a Coca-Cola in her hand. Feet on his desk, she began sipping at the drink.

Todd entered, picked her up by the arm, and gestured her out into the corridor. They walked down the hallway together, and still without a word, he marched her along into a deserted office.

"He sort of plunked me on the couch," Elizabeth recalled. Then he pulled up a chair and started to talk. He said a lot of things. Among them he said that he was in love with her. He wanted her. They were just right for each other and so on. All during his spiel he did not even touch her hand.

At the end of it he looked at her and said, "Don't horse around. You're going to marry me."

It was, according to Elizabeth, "like sitting in quicksand and seeing it coming up all over you and not being able to move."

"Jeez," she thought, "I've got to get away from this man." And she walked out on him.

At least, that was Elizabeth's version of the scene. However the scene was played, the intent was the same. Even Hedda Hopper, she of the laundered tongue, wrote that Todd played the scene in typical Todd-ese: "From now on, you'll know nobody but me." "Only," Hopper elaborated, "he didn't say 'know.' "

Elizabeth had to think. The best place to think was on the set. And besides, she was scheduled to do the location scenes on *Raintree County*. By now Clift had recovered enough from his plastic surgery to continue.

Back in Hollywood, Todd reached out and touched his someone every couple of hours wherever she was. Sometimes more than twice a day Elizabeth was called to the telephone to receive a long-distance call from him. One call lasted three hours. Once they were both talking at five a.m. in the morning.

What Todd was best at was selling himself. He sold himself to Elizabeth. When she came home from location, she began to see him regularly. By now Elizabeth was very chary of publicity. She insisted on secrecy when they went out. To assume that Elizabeth Taylor, known to every movie fan in

114   BILL ADLER

the world, and Mike Todd, known to every news-
paper reader of the age, could go incognito up and
down the street was a joke of the broadest order.

Todd took her to a cocktail party where a room-
ful of strangers ogled the two of them as they swept
up—Elizabeth in her usual regal costume, and
Todd in his swaggering, Damon Runyan getup.
Todd introduced her with a sweep of the hand as
Miss Lizzie Schwartzkopf—German for "Black-
head."

During the ensuing few moments one of Todd's
show biz friends kept looking at Ms. Schwartzkopf
with some interest. "You know," he told her, "you
look a lot like Elizabeth Taylor, only heavier."

Todd slapped Elizabeth's bottom. "Lizzie, I told
you you're getting fat!"

Perelman noted, "They were not an incongruous
couple because they were both so showbiz."

Todd squired her all around the country, setting
up future engagements for *Around the World.* An
observer recalled seeing them one day in Province-
town.

"There was a buzz coming down the street. People were staring before they knew that it was Elizabeth Taylor. It was an extraordinary physical phenomenon, that's the only way to describe it
. . . those incredible blue eyes, raking the horizon."

And Elizabeth didn't look as short as usual, because Todd was short too.

"There was never any second proposal after the
first one," Elizabeth recounted. Todd sent a special
plane to fly her to New York. "When the plane
landed, he was out on the field waiting, and I ran

down the steps into his arms and we kissed for the first time."

October 4 the news broke via the gossip columns that Elizabeth intended to divorce Michael Wilding. There was a great deal of clucking from the arbiters of social mores—Hopper, Parsons, and Graham. The Republic trembled, but then subsided. The papers were filed on November 14.

But meanwhile—down at the Todd-AO Ranch —*Around the World in 80 Days* opened at its premier in New York City on October 17. At the height of its festivities, Todd announced that he and Elizabeth were going to be married.

And, simultaneously, she exhibited the diamond engagement ring that proved Mike Todd wasn't just talking through his hat.

"The diamond is one inch across and five-eighths of an inch deep," one reporter said, "and nothing like it has been seen since the Maharajas went out of business." Estimates of its cost ranged from $92,000 to $100,000 and more.

One observer remarked that it was probably one of the most tasteless rings ever viewed in public. "It was all mad and marvelous!" Elizabeth recalled.

Just after the Wilding divorce papers were filed, with Elizabeth requesting $250 a month in child support but no alimony, Elizabeth and Todd flew to Miami. They had been invited by Lord Beaverbrook, the British newspaper magnate, to dinner in Nassau. Todd chartered a cumbersome sailing houseboat to make the crossing to the island. On the return, Elizabeth took a header on the steep ladder and slammed to the deck on her spine.

Todd flew her up to New York and checked her

into Harkness Pavilion at the Columbia-Presby-
terian Medical Center. There the roentgenograms
showed a mass of crushed spinal discs. She un-
derwent a five-hour operation. The discs were removed and pieces of bone from her hip, her pelvis,
and a bone bank were grafted in their new place to
form a new six-inch-long construction. The minute
she came out of surgery and opened her eyes she
saw Todd.

"Where's my diamond ring?" she asked him.
Todd told the story to reporters with typical pan-
ache.

Because her spine was in such a precarious state,
she was advised not to undertake any more preg-
nancies.

Todd wouldn't leave her alone. It was too complicated coming in each day at visiting hours. Todd
moved into the hospital, renting a room himself.
Then he had an aide purchase a group of original
oils by Monet, Renoir and Pissarro and hang them
on the three walls of her room so she could see
them from her bed.

Todd sent for Peggy Rutledge and Virginia
Streeter, another of Elizabeth's assistants, to help
Elizabeth in the hospital. Todd never got along
with either Peggy or Virginia. They left Elizabeth's
service during her year with Todd.

Two months later she finally left the hospital in
January, still confined to the wheelchair. Her
divorce was not final until February. But Todd was
in a hurry.

He had gone to great lengths to arrange the
Wilding-Taylor divorce in Acapulco, but at the last
minute everything got screwed up when a civil

court judge rejected the petition. He had already drawn up the papers, but suddenly decided that he could not sign them because of public opinion. Todd blew his top, started pulling strings in higher places, and quite suddenly everything was smoothed out and the divorce was granted on January 30.

Three days later, on February 2, the mayor of Acapulco married Elizabeth and Todd in a ceremony at which everyone who was anyone was present. For example:

Michael Wilding was there; he was responsible for making all the wedding arrangements. Todd's best friend, a young singer named Eddie Fisher, was there, singing the wedding serenade. Mrs. Fisher, actress Debbie Reynolds, was a bridesmaid. Even Sara and Francis Taylor were there. The bride could barely hobble up the aisle, but she made it.

Cantinflas, a famed Mexican actor whose real name is Mario Gonzalez, helped Todd carry her around after that where she needed to go. After the wedding there was a gauche, absolutely unbelievable reception, including fireworks watched by the guests from a grandstand. The grandstand was decorated with red satin bunting and fresh orchids. The entire sky lighted up with bursting lights initialing E. T. and M. T. with two big intertwined hearts between.

Naturally the story hit all the front pages, complete with descriptions of the festivities. Not a single item was missed. Except one, perhaps. Nobody made any comment on the fact that Elizabeth was pregnant again.

"Even by Hollywood standards this marriage seems to be for keeps," said comedian Ernie Kovacs. "It should last forever—or at least three years."

It was a sadly prophetic remark. The marriage lasted for only a little over one year—384 days, to be exact.

From the start, they traveled everywhere together. Elizabeth did not do any picture work until the end of the year. 1957 was for *Around the World*. To publicize it Todd spent money with abandon. They went everywhere. They made love. They laughed at the world. And they fought each other with spats that were supercolossal.

"Look," Todd told one friend. "This gal's been looking for trouble all her life. Now she's found somebody who can give it to her."

"When Elizabeth flies into a tantrum," he told another, "I fly into a bigger one. We fight because we love it. When she's mad she looks so beautiful that I want to take her in my arms and smother her with kisses. But I control myself—I fight—because it's so much fun to make up again."

The London bash for *Around the World* was a mind-boggler. Todd rented Battersea Fun Fair for a celebration following the London opening of the movie. He hired scores of red London buses to haul the people from the theater to the park.

Vivien Leigh and her husband Laurence Olivier rode the Rotor, and the Duchess of Marlborough ate a hamburger out of a paper napkin. It was a hell of a party. It rained, as it always did in London, but Todd handed out umbrellas and plastic raincoats to everybody. Aly Khan got a ladies' white one. "I thought I'd heard everything," Todd said later, "but one guy—the descendant of a former prime minister, too—well, he came and complained that his free coat didn't fit!"

Sixteen separate orchestras played while chefs from seven nations dished out hundreds of pounds of fish and chips and seven bars dispensed champagne, hard liquor, beer and pop. A man carrying a tray loaded with champagne was hailed by an English aristocrat as a waiter. It was Eddie Fisher.

On the boat returning to the States Elizabeth went into premature labor. The ship's doctor anesthetized her and stopped the labor. Once in New York, she went into Harkness again while Todd opened the show in Minneapolis. They spent the summer in a twenty-three room Westport estate Todd rented. But on July 28 she was back in Harkness, again in premature labor.

On August 3 she checked out, but next day collapsed in Westport. An ambulance rushed her back to Harkness and two days later a team of eight doctors said they could wait no longer, although Elizabeth pleaded with them: "Don't take her. She's not cooked yet."

Elizabeth Frances Todd was delivered via Caesarean section on August 6, and came into the world at four pounds, fourteen ounces (also reported as five pounds, nine ounces). She did not breathe for fourteen and a half minutes, but then she came around. A jubilant Todd viewed her and was ecstatic when she proved to be perfectly healthy. After taking one look at her, he said, "With her around, I fear for the next generation of males." She spent the first two months of her life in an oxygen tent.

Later on, clowning around for photographers at

the Westport house, Todd presented Liza—as she would always be called—with a gold hair brush. "It would have been platinum," he told her in Todd-ese, "but your mother would have said I was spoiling you."

When Michael Wilding Jr. dropped a rattle into the crib on her, Todd soothed her screams and tears. "May you never suffer a worse hurt."

The old energy was bubbling over again, and Todd felt the need to celebrate. Besides, it was time to honor the first anniversary of *Around the World*. "Fine," said Elizabeth. "A small, dignified party."

"Right!" said Todd, and rented Madison Square Garden, inviting 18,000 guests. In October, the marquee over the Garden read:

A LITTLE PRIVATE PARTY TONIGHT

It was chaos inside. There were: 15,000 doughnuts; 15,000 hot dogs; 10,000 slices of pizza; 10,000 egg rolls; 2,200 gallons of vichyssoise; a 14-foot-high birthday cake made from 2,000 eggs and 1,000 pounds of cake mix.

There were gifts, including: six automobiles; one Cessna airplane; 25 hi fi sets; champagne; 20 automatic toasters; 10 ladies' revolvers; 10 hot-water bags; 50 elephant bells; 500 phonograph records; 400 boxes of imported cigars; 35 hundred-pound barbells; and 50 harmonicas.

Thousands of gatecrashers broke in, milling about until the party turned into a howling, clawing, enraged mob. Food vanished before guests could fight their way to the tables. Waiters scalped watered-down champagne at $10 a bottle. The party played on television. CBS-TV paid Todd $300,000 for the right to film it.

"I've worked in war zones, so I should have been prepared," one commentator said. "But this scene of utter chaos defied me. Perhaps it can best be compared to mass battlefield desertions by both the winning and losing sides."

In the midst of the total confusion, Todd grabbed hold of a microphone and announced over the loudspeakers: "I hoped things would run smoother than they did, but some nights are better than others."

Elizabeth and Todd vanished before the fiasco wore down. In genuine privacy they toasted one another and laughed at what was happening back at the Garden.

By November 15, Todd and Elizabeth were in Hong Kong. There Elizabeth was stricken with appendicitis. When they returned to the States she eventually had an appendectomy on December 17 at Cedars of Lebanon, staying a week. Again Todd took the connecting suite.

In January, the Todds were in London en route to Moscow. Todd ferried his 12-passenger plane, *The Lucky Liz,* to England. There they jet-setted about from place to place, wherever they wanted to party. The journey to Moscow, however, took place in a Soviet jet.

Elizabeth was commissioned to write a column for International News Service on her travels. In Moscow, she wrote: "I was told the Georgians and most Russians are very hospitable. If you admire something they give it to you." She went and admired the Russian crown jewels. "I stood there and admired and admired them—but nothing happened. I saw the jewels that the czars kept for their horses. That made me wish I were a horse."

In spite of the fact that Todd kept saying he wanted Elizabeth around him always, it was he who finally worked out the arrangements for her to star as Maggie the Cat in *Cat on a Hot Tin Roof,* to be made by Pandro S. Berman at M.G.M.

And Elizabeth agreed. M.G.M. had paid $600,000 to Tennessee Williams for the screen rights, and wanted to cut the budget elsewhere, to bring it in for $1,000,000. So Technicolor was out, black and white was in. Richard Brooks, the director, ran into Todd one afternoon at the studio.

"What's the matter, kid?" Todd asked.

"They're making it in black and white."

"You think that's stupid?"

"Here they are, supposedly a wealthy family in the South and here's one of the most beautiful women in the world, and it's going to be in black and white!"

Todd went upstairs. Some minutes later Eddie Mannix, Bennie Thau, and Laurence Weingarten —top execs at M.G.M—appeared and found Brooks.

"Why don't you make it in color?" one suggested.

It was Elizabeth's first time to play opposite Paul Newman. Like Clift and Dean and a lot of others, Newman was another Method actor. During the runthrough, Newman was appalled at Elizabeth's acting. He drew aside Brooks and said:

"What's going to happen? There's nothing there."

"Paul," Brooks countered, "she doesn't work in that way. You watch. When we're ready to go, she'll be *there!*"

She was. As Brooks recalled, she came on like Gangbusters. But by the second week of shooting, Elizabeth came down with a virus. She was scheduled to fly to New York with Todd on Saturday to receive an award at the Friars Testimonial Dinner at the Waldorf-Astoria in New York. Thirteen hundred people would be attending.

But she was in bed on Friday, with a temperature of 102. She wanted to get up and go with him, but he wouldn't take her. Elizabeth's physician, Dr. Rexford Kennamer, agreed with Todd. The weather was bad, and worse was on its way.

A lot of Todd's friends turned him down on the flight. He wound up going with Art Cohn, a writer who was doing a biography of him. Joe E. Lewis, Kirk Douglas, Kurt Frings, and even Joseph L. Mankiewicz all declined. Cohn was also scripting *Don Quixote,* Todd's next oeuvre.

But Todd found it difficult to leave the house. He played with the children, Christopher and Michael, and they all got into the big sunken bathtub and doused each other with water. Then it came time for him to go. He kissed Elizabeth goodbye and went downstairs. Then he was back again, holding her, kissing her again.

It was almost a kind of premonition that their time was running out.

"I'm too happy," he said. "I'm so afraid something's going to happen. I'm too happy."

Then he left again. But not for good. He was back in, and saying goodbye.

But finally he did leave. *The Lucky Liz* took off from Burbank. And Elizabeth found it impossible to sleep. Todd had promised to call her from Albuquerque where they were scheduled to land for refueling. Elizabeth was by the telephone from six o'clock on. But he didn't call.

By seven o'clock, there was still no call. Elizabeth called Richard Hanley, once Louis B. Mayer's personal secretary and now one of Mike Todd's assistants. "It's so strange that Mike hasn't let me hear from him," she said. "Do you think anything could have happened? It was such a miserable night."

The fact was that *The Lucky Liz* was no more. At 2 a.m. in the morning, seven thousand feet above the Zuni Mountains in New Mexico, the wings of the ship had iced up, and the plane had failed to get above the storm. It had crashed in the badlands.

At eight-thirty in the morning Elizabeth looked up from her bed to find Richard Hanley and Dr. Rexford Kennamar standing there. Elizabeth sat up in bed looking at them in the doorway, thinking at first that her doctor had come to see how she was.

But she could tell by the looks on their faces that something had happened. It was not hard to guess what. Elizabeth shook her head and screamed "No" before she had even heard, and jumped out of bed. She ran downstairs and all through the house and out into the street before Kennamar could catch up with her and bring her back.

Then he knocked her out with a sleeping pill.

"No, no, no—it just can't be," she wept. "He'll phone me soon—he always does when he's out of town."

And she drifted off.

CHAPTER EIGHT
Elisheba Rachel

It did not take long for news of Mike Todd's death to make the rounds. He had scores of friends. Most of them called briefly at the house or sent messages of condolence. One of them, Eddie Fisher, stayed close to Elizabeth's side. On the morning when Elizabeth was sedated, Fisher's wife, M.G.M. actress Debbie Reynolds, came to collect the Wilding-Todd children to take them home with her.

The Fishers were close to the Todds. A pop singer in the style of Bing Crosby and Frank Sinatra, Fisher had tried out once for a part in one of Todd's musicals. He hadn't been hired, but Todd remembered him and liked him for his boyish grin and youthful exuberance.

Fisher began hanging around Todd, watching him and admiring him. Todd thrived on that kind of adulation. Fisher began looking up to Todd as a kind of surrogate father. Todd liked to think of Fisher as the son he never had. In that way there was a pseudo-father-son relationship between the two men.

The Fishers had two children, the oldest named Carrie Francis Fisher, and the youngest, born only three weeks before Todd's death, named Todd Emmanuel Fisher after his father's idol. It was only proper, it seemed to everyone, that Fisher should stand closely by the grieving Widow Todd in the stressful days that followed.

They were not easy ones. But somehow Elizabeth got through them. So did the man who had lost his surrogate father.

Todd's funeral in Chicago was a nightmare of howling fans—fans of both Elizabeth and of Todd —of unsuppressed violence, of helpless police battling unruly mobs. Howard Hughes sent a TWA plane and crew (he owned the company) to fly Elizabeth there. At the Drake Hotel the funeral party spread out over fifteen rooms.

On the day of the funeral, Elizabeth was hustled into a limousine, heavily sedated, for the trip to the grave site. She was wearing a small black veil and a black hat Todd had given her. The streets were mobbed. Going past a factory she saw two girls hanging out of a window, one yelling: "Dig that crazy widow's veil!"

At the cemetery the scene resembled a World Series game, with people draped over gravestones, hanging from trees, and tramping over the entire area: ten thousand of them according to an official police estimate. It was bitter chill, the wind blowing junk food wrappers and other debris across the grass.

When the limo pulled up, the crowd surged across the way, surrounding the funeral party like some kind of hysterical mob.

The coffin was finally lowered into the grave and the crowd responded with yelling and shouting. Elizabeth asked to be alone to pray. It was almost impossible. As she knelt and closed her eyes the mob that had been pushing against the police lines all day broke through and surrounded her as if they wanted to destroy her.

Her brother Howard was holding her. The screaming fans began ripping at her head, trying to tear off the hat and veil for souvenirs. The two of them fought their way through the crowd back to the limousine. Finally they got into the limousine and Elizabeth screamed to go, but the driver was missing. They saw him fighting his way through the mob. Fans were at the window, peering in, climbing onto the car. They began to rock it.

Elizabeth almost went out of her mind. Finally the driver forced his way inside and they drove out of the cemetery with the mob surging about them "like insects," Elizabeth recalled.

The widow did not respond as rapidly as some might. For weeks she prevented her maid from changing the bedsheets in the house. Elizabeth did not clean out the closets at all. She kept looking at Todd's things, and remembering.

Suddenly she had had enough. Everything was packed away. She was ready to face the future without him.

"You have to watch not to build a shrine," she said.

Her next step was not a difficult one to make. In fact, Todd had made the decision for her when he had persuaded her to act in *Cat on a Hot Tin Roof.* Only three scenes had been shot from the movie when Todd was killed. Nevertheless, Todd had watched all the rushes with her.

"You've never been so good in your life," he told her. "Maybe you won't win the Academy Award for *Raintree County,* but you'll win it next year for this one."

She called Richard Brooks and told him she would return to work. "The only reason I want to do it is because of Mike," she said. "Mike liked me in this picture, and I want to finish it for him."

And so on the morning of April 14, Elizabeth drove to the studio lot at seven a.m. in her black Dual Ghia sports car with the telephone labeled "Hers" on the dial. It was one of Todd's last gifts to her, matching his Rolls Royce with "His" written on it.

After an hour and a half in makeup, where her makeup man observed that "She seemed just the same as usual," she walked over to costume and slipped out of her black slacks and sweater into a white chiffon summer dress with a V-neck, white satin belt and full skirt. They had to take in the dress; she had lost eight pounds.

Then she drove through the studio streets to Stage 23 and filming began once again. She was greeted by all hands: Burl Ives, playing Big Daddy Pollitt; Judith Anderson, playing Big Mama; Jack Carson, playing Grooper; and Paul Newman, playing Brick.

When it came to rehearsing a scene, Brooks was surprised and concerned to detect a slight stammer in her speech, both on the set and off. She was also apparently quite weak from lack of food. When she tried to lift a suitcase off a bed as her first piece of business, she was unable to do it naturally. The scene had to be reshot later on.

In a dinner scene at Big Daddy's birthday party, Brooks forced her to eat real food, doing retakes again and again. She began to taste the food and to *want* to eat. Within days she was almost back to normal again.

"She was remarkable," recalled Laurence Weingarten, the picture's producer. "She was working on a string for the first two weeks after her return, but you can't see a flaw in her performance."

Friends liked to compare her courage in returning to work in three weeks with the courage of another Hollywood stalwart—Clark Gable. It took Gable six weeks to return after Carole Lombard's death. "She's a practical girl, and you can't kid her. She also has guts."

The plot of *Cat* concerns the relationship between Maggie (Elizabeth) and Brick (Newman). Newman is Ives's favorite son, but a disturbed man who can't seem to find his way in life after a promising start in school. In the Broadway play, the character is a homosexual, struggling to achieve a relationship with his wife. In the movie, the homosexuality is blurred over, making the charter a kind of lush grieving over the death of a friend.

The key scene is Maggie's demand to know what

it is that is troubling Brick and ruining their marriage. In it, Elizabeth did the best work she had done to date, hurling out her frustration and agony in charring speeches—all photographed in one long scene with no cuts or shifts of view.

Todd had been right in his appraisal of Elizabeth's work. It was superior and worthy of an Academy Award. She was nominated for the award, but did not win. There were reasons for this, to be explained later.

"Elizabeth Taylor has a major credit with her portrayal of Maggie," wrote *Variety*. "The frustrations and desires, both as a person and as a woman, the warmth and understanding she molds, the loveliness that is more than a well-turned nose—all these are part of a well-accented perceptive interpretation. That she performed in this manner under the stress of recent tragedy makes her performance certain to provoke conversation."

Bosley Crowther of the *New York Times:* "Miss Taylor is terrific as a panting, impatient wife, wanting the love of her husband as sincerely as she wants his inheritance." Even *Time* admitted: "Elizabeth Taylors plays with surprising sureness." And *Life* said: "Elizabeth Taylor gives the best performance of her career as Maggie the Cat. . . . It is a volatile role of a rejected wife who fights tenaciously to win back her husband's love."

Her next motion picture would be another Tennessee Williams adaptation, this one *Suddenly Last Summer,* another long hard look at homosexuality and excesses—in this case, cannibalism. But meanwhile she was trying desperately to find her way back to a kind of personal lifestyle that would work. And she was as curious as anybody else about where her future lay. Would she marry again? Would she devote herself to her career?

The consensus was that she would marry once again. She began to be seen going out with Arthur Loew, Jr., a long-time friend whom she had known since she was fourteen. She traveled to Tucson to visit Loew's sister, married and living there. She also took the three children to visit her old friends the Stewart Grangers, now on their ranch near Nogales. And, on the way to Europe where she intended to take a short vacation, she was seen for a short time with Eddie Fisher, Mike Todd's protégé.

That meeting was a pivotal one.

Edward Jack Fisher was a Philadelphia boy, born in 1928, just four years before Elizabeth. He had a boyish face and grin, and grew up with a dream of being a big singing star. He had an untrained baritone that eventually earned him a number of golden records.

But Eddie Fisher was not Mike Todd. He was primarily a singer, not a publicist or a showman like Todd. His career became controlled by a promoter and agent named Milton Blackstone, born Schwartzstein.

Blackstone worked for Jennie Grossinger, and it was in the Borscht Belt that he found Fisher and agreed to help him become a singer. After several initial appearances arranged by Blackstone, Fisher found to his sorrow that producers weren't breaking down the door with offers. He decided to quit.

But Blackstone shook his head. He now began to "create" Eddie Fisher.

He wangled several appearances, and then made sure that Fisher was present when Eddie Cantor visited the Catskills during the summer. Blackstone introduced them, and Cantor agreed to take on Fisher if the audience liked him. Blackstone packed the tables with a hired claque. Cantor was a wily old pro who knew what was happening, but he took Fisher on anyway.

Fisher moved up and up finally becoming the star of *Coke Time* in 1953, and parlayed that television and radio show into a number of golden records through the next few years. His popularity surged when he married Debbie Reynolds, a "cleancut" American girl, known as "America's Sweetheart" some years after Mary Pickford surrendered the title.

"Never have I seen a more patriotic match than these two clean-cut, clean-living youngsters," wrote Hedda Hopper. "When I think of them, I see flags flying and hear bands playing."

Unknown to the public, Fisher and Debbie had problems from the beginning of the marriage. These stemmed from basic incompatibility and perhaps a health regimen developed by Dr. Max Jacobson, a highly respected New York physician of the 1950s. Later these "injections" of vitamins and unnamed drugs—pep pills—all became suspect when they had destroyed the careers of several promising show business people, including that of Milton Blackstone. At the time America was a pill-popping nation with little concern for the effects of these regimens.

Debbie Reynolds bore two children for Fisher, the second, as has been mentioned, named after Mike Todd. Fisher's career then began to sink with the change in music styles engineered by Elvis Presley and later the English Beatles. Fisher found it difficult to cope. But Debbie's career flourished. With Todd, at least Fisher had someone to respect. After Todd married Elizabeth Taylor, the couples were frequently seen in public together.

One waiter at Chasen's in Beverly Hills described the ritual whereby whatever Todd selected, Fisher would ask for exactly the same. Fisher even ate the way Todd did—fast. Fisher had never considered himself a carbon copy of Todd, though. "Maybe I had adopted some of Mike's superficial characteristics, but I wasn't trying to step into his shoes," he wrote. "I was still me."

Liz Taylor, though, was something else. She had a mind of her own. Nobody dared to tell her what to have!

Fisher's marriage to Debbie had disintegrated long before Todd's death. The marriage itself had been a bad mistake. When their engagement was first announced, Fisher's record sales had dropped off. Actually Fisher was not wholly his own man. Eddie Fisher was the RamRod Company, formed by the partnership of Eddie Fisher and Milton Blackstone. Others bought into the company and helped make decisions. Show business was tricky: if a talent didn't do the right thing, the public could turn against the star. Because Eddie Fisher appealed to young and squealing teen-agers, his youth and single status were important. His advisors warned him about marriage.

"You were anxious to get married but you haven't found the right girl," they said. "Your engagement is a million-dollar mistake."

Fisher stalled. Debbie was puzzled. Fisher was afraid to break it off with her. "You've got to go through with it now," Blackstone told him. Fisher was working in New York. When he tried to move to Hollywood to be with Debbie, the NBC-TV brass refused to let him go. The resulting hassle confused and upset him. But he set the date for the marriage anyway.

They were married at Grossinger's. Once it was a *fait accompli,* Fisher's advisors went along with it. The Fishers became "America's Sweethearts," and the catchword was played up by Fisher's flak.

But once Debbie had some say in the matter of her husband's career, she advised him to drop all his advisors. She didn't get along with them. In addition to that, she was appalled at his regular "injections" from Jacobson.

When Fisher tried to drop Jacobson, he got into trouble with Blackstone. And when Debbie pressured him again about firing his advisors, he pretended to act, but actually did nothing. Instead of staying at home, he started hanging around with his cronies in nightclubs and at gambling tables. Sometimes he was tossing money around all night.

Nor did he discontinue Jacobson's injections. It was at this time, when Fisher continued to hide out from Debbie, they finally began to think about divorce. Almost coincidental with this decision, Debbie found herself pregnant for the second time. It was obviously the wrong time for a splitup. So, for a while, the couple continued to act as if they were still "America's Sweethearts."

Once Todd Emmanuel Fisher was born, the divorce again became imminent. And that was the critical stage of the Fisher marriage when Todd was killed in the crash of *The Lucky Liz*.

Fisher was in New York seeing sponsors for a new TV show when Elizabeth ran into him on her way to Europe. And then one thing lead to another and. . . .

Item: Elizabeth and Eddie Fisher were seen at the Blue Angel with Eva Marie Saint. The story hit the papers, with pictures of Fisher and the Widow Todd "dancing it up," in Earl Wilson's words.

Item: Elizabeth, Fisher, Blackstone and the entire entourage spent the Labor Day weekend at Grossinger's in the Catskills. "The story-book marriage of Eddie Fisher and Debbie Reynolds skidded on a series of curves yesterday—Liz Taylor's," announced the *New York Daily Mirror* with glee. The Fisher marriage had hit "a snag—in the graceful shape . . . of sultry Liz Taylor," said the *New York Daily News*, evoking the same metaphorical reference.

Item: The two were seen at the Harwyn Club. Flashbulbs. Column notices.

Item: Whatever happened to that European
tour?

Item: September 9: "Eddie Fisher Romance with
Liz Taylor Denied." In tabloid jargon, that meant
that what was denied was true.

Item: Debbie Reynolds stated: "I am so shocked
that such stories would be printed that I won't even
dignify them with any comments. Eddie and Liz
are very good friends."

Item: September 10. Headlines: "Debbie and
Eddie Feud."

The feud was real. The Fishers were heard to
row in their white brick cottage by the fifteen reporters lounging around on the front lawn waiting
for quotes. "What's the matter with you, anyway?"
screeched Debbie at one point; the scribes scrib-
bled it down. Inside, according to one source, Debbie was following her husband about, red-faced
with anger and screaming at him.

Finally Elizabeth returned to the Coast. News of
her flight leaked and the airport was acrawl with
reporters. Her statement when it came was typical
cool Taylor: "I have nothing to say but hello."

Item: Now M.G.M. got out the mimeograph
machine and a statement was forthcoming. "A separation exists between Eddie and Debbie," the official announcement said, reminiscent of Elizabeth
Taylor's earlier "announcements." "No further action is being taken at this time." Headlines: "Eddie
and Debbie Tell Separation."

The roof of the world simply caved in on the two
lovers. From the vantage point of the 1980s, seeing
across lifestyles through the 1970s and the 1960s,

the attitude of the public at that time is simply incredible. But people forget that Ingrid Bergman, who dropped her husband and "took up" with Roberto Rossellini, was actually blacklisted by Hollywood for a number of years before she was allowed back.

What happened to Ingrid Bergman happened to Elizabeth Taylor and Eddie Fisher in 1958. The media, reflecting as always the current morality of the public they serve, heaped gobs and gobs of vitriol and rage onto the two "sinners." Elizabeth was transformed overnight from the Widow Todd into a "viper," a "harlot," a "cannibal," a "barbarian," a "destroyer," a "Jezebel," and so on. It was suggested by a minister that she be burned in effigy. Fan magazines wrote that their readers should boycott her movies. She was vilified, as was Fisher, by all the people who had been eager to celebrate her widowhood weeks before.

Elizabeth was stunned at the reaction. She had moved out of her house and taken up a suite in the Beverly Hills Hotel. Smarting under what she considered to be overkill by the media, she stayed out of sight until things could blow over. During that period she made up her mind. She would marry Fisher and to hell with her critics.

Eddie was in seclusion too. He was living with an old friend. Debbie was staying with her friends Marge and Gower Champion.

By December 4, things had cooled off enough for Debbie to file for divorce. On February 19, the decree came through. She got a million dollars, and child support. So much for the Fisher-Reynolds marriage.

The divorce, to be final in a few months, left the way clear for Elizabeth to marry Eddie Fisher. But first there were other problems that had nothing to do with Fisher, except tangentially. Once again it was finances.

Although Elizabeth had inherited Mike Todd's estate, she was hardly a wealthy widow. Neither Todd nor Elizabeth owned a house. In the last year of his life Todd spent about $1.5 million. Elizabeth inherited 50 percent of the Michael Todd Company; the other half went to Michael Todd, Jr. The company's main asset was *Around the World in 80 Days* and the picture owed United Artists as distributors a cool $2 million; CBS, owner of 8 percent, about $1 million; and Paramount Pictures, another $750,000.

Clearly, Elizabeth had to go back to work. She had three children, two parents, a personal staff, and a lifestyle to keep up. If she married Fisher, he had alimony to pay. On January 6, 1959, Fisher was notified that his NBC television show was being cancelled. And Happy New Year!

During her marriage to Todd, Elizabeth had confessed to him that she had often thought of converting to Judaism. Todd was skeptical. He thought she was simply talking. But he indulged her whim and warned her: "Be slow, be deliberate, be careful. Don't do it on account of me. In ten years, *then* do it."

But when he died, she remembered her resolve. She studied for nine months, going to the temple regularly and was converted on March 2, 1959, by Rabbi Max Nussbaum at Temple Israel, Hollywood.

"She was a good pupil," he said. "She has a good understanding of Jewish life and has read extensively in Jewish history. She is very intelligent."

Accompanied by Dr. Rex Kennamer, Dick Hanley, and her mother and father, she became Elisheba (Hebrew for Elizabeth) Rachel. "I picked the Reform philosophy because it has a gentleness, an understanding, a largeness that makes me feel quiet and calm and gentle inside," she said.

Immediately all her films were banned in Egypt and boycotted in all Arab countries in Africa and the Middle East.

She kept to her resolve and on May 12, 1959, she was married to Eddie Fisher, with her stepson, Mike Todd, Jr., acting as best man, and her brother Howard's wife, Mara, as matron of honor. The ceremony took place at the Temple Beth Sholom in Las Vegas, where Fisher was performing at the Tropicana.

The newlyweds flew to L.A. and then on to New York. There they spent a night at the Waldorf, flying on to Spain for their honeymoon. In Spain they boarded the rented 200-ton yacht *Olnico* and set sail from Barcelona for a long Mediterranean honeymoon.

In Spain on the Costa Brava Elizabeth reported for some location shooting for *Suddenly Last Summer,* and then went on to London to work at Shepperton Studios where most of the picture was made. The picture was not without its problems. Although Elizabeth loved being reunited with her old friend Montgomery Clift, she was startled to see the personality change in him. He had become more heavily addicted to drugs and alcohol than at any time previously. In some instances he was unable to remember his lines, and found it difficult to concentrate on what was happening on the set.

Director Joseph L. Mankiewicz was forced to photograph his scenes in short takes—a phrase here, a sentence there—in order to get the scene on film. Producer Sam Spiegel conferred with Mankiewicz and suggested dumping Clift, but Elizabeth wouldn't have it.

The rest of the cast was memorable: Katharine Hepburn played Mrs. Violet Venable; Mercedes McCambridge was Mrs. Holly; Clift played Dr. Cukrowicz; and Albert Dekker was Dr. Hockstader. Elizabeth was in the key role of Catherine Holly.

The script had been adapted from Tennessee Williams' one-act play by Gore Vidal and Williams. It toned down the homosexual references in the original. But the cannibalism was still there, and the sordid evidence of homosexuality was left for anyone who wished to see it.

Structurally, the picture was talky, with long speeches, none as long as Elizabeth's final harangue. The plot progression depends on her final revelation of what really happened "suddenly, last summer"—a grisly incident which has been buried in her mind because of its utter horror.

As Clift unlocks the memory in her mind, and as she sees it again and reveals it not only to herself but to the rest of the cast, she becomes the focal point of the entire drama for an unbelievable twelve pages of monologue.

It took two days to shoot that scene, but Elizabeth's speech went on and on with repeats from different camera angles.

"I ended the scene down on the floor screaming —and I couldn't stop crying even after it was finished," she recalled.

Mankiewicz described her key scene as an "aria" —"as long and difficult a speech, I venture, as any ever attempted on the screen."

It was Hepburn this time who took up the cause of Clift, inviting him to spend weekends with her at a country house near London. She tried to get him to give up the drugs and alcohol, but she couldn't.

When the picture was wrapped, Hepburn visited Mankiewicz.

"There's nothing more you're going to need me for?" she asked. "No looping, no pick-up shots, no retakes?"

"I've got it all, Kate," he said. "And it's great. *You're* great. What *is* all this?"

"I just want to leave you with this," Hepburn said, and spat in Mankiewicz's face.

She visited Spiegel's office, and spat again.

To the world at large, she elaborated: "I didn't spit just for Monty Clift! I spit at them for the way they treated *me*."

Not all the critics were happy with the movie. "A preposterous and monotonous potpourri of incest, homosexuality, psychiatry, and, so help me, cannibalism," grumbled the *New Yorker*.

"Elizabeth Taylor is rightly roiled as the niece, but her wallow of agony at the climax is sheer histrionic showing off." Thus Bosley Crowther of the *New York Times*.

But others saw her work in a different light.

"And if there were ever any doubts about the ability of Miss Taylor to express complex and devious emotions, to deliver a flexible and deep performance, this film ought to remove them," wrote Paul V. Beckley for the *New York Herald Tribune*.

"Miss Taylor is most effective in her later scenes, although these scenes have been robbed of their original theatricality in transfer from stage to screen," said *Variety*.

"The playing is dogged (Clift), arrestingly mannered (Hepburn), and courageously whole-hearted (Taylor). But the work itself remains a sickly fantasy." So said *Sight and Sound*.

On September 1 Elizabeth got a call in her suite at the Dorchester Hotel. Her husband answered. It was Walter Wanger calling about *Cleopatra*—a movie that had been discussed before several times. Wanger wanted Elizabeth for the lead. Elizabeth was amused.

"Tell him I'll do it for a million dollars against ten percent of the gross."

It was a throw-away line. She forgot all about it. Fisher dutifully repeated it to Wanger.

Twentieth Century-Fox accepted it. Elizabeth was astonished. She couldn't do the picture immediately. There was one stumbling block: one last picture for M.G.M. to fulfill her extended contract. And it was a thing called *Butterfield 8*, from a short story by John O'Hara about a New York call girl.

CHAPTER NINE
Death and Resurrection

During the most powerful surge of public antipathy toward Elizabeth Taylor because of her involvement with Eddie Fisher, the 1958 Academy Awards were distributed. Sure enough, although Elizabeth had been nominated for her role of Maggie the Cat, she lost out to Susan Hayward for her role in *I Want to Live!*

And with the public still not too happy with her during her early married months as Mrs. Edward Jack Fisher, her nomination for her role in *Suddenly Last Summer* also did not win her the Oscar the next year. The Oscar went to Simone Signoret for *Room at the Top*.

By now Elizabeth was quite sure she would never win, no matter what kind of role she played. With such an honor on her Impossible List, she decided to concentrate on another aspect of her career: money.

There had been some skirmishing at Twentieth Century-Fox over the *Cleopatra* role. Spyros P. Skouras, head of the studio since the departure of

Darryl F. Zanuck, didn't want Elizabeth Taylor. He wanted Susan Hayward. Or, failing Hayward, maybe Brigitte Bardot, Marilyn Monroe, Jennifer Jones, Kim Novak, Audrey Hepburn, Sophia Loren, Gina Lollobrigida, or Suzy Parker.

"She'll be too much trouble," Skouras warned Wanger, speaking of Elizabeth. Another Fox bigwig snorted: "Who needs a Liz Taylor? Any hundred-dollar-a-week girl can play Cleopatra."

Over Skouras's all but dead body, Wanger won out and the contract was signed—the most expensive contract ever signed by any film actor to that date. And then M.G.M. suddenly woke up. She couldn't play *Cleopatra* until she worked out her last deal with M.G.M.!

And so, Elizabeth realized that to get the million offered for *Cleopatra,* she would have to play in *Butterfield 8* for $100,000. Unfortunately it was all spelled out in black and white in her contract.

Pandro S. Berman, her producer, explained: "First of all, she was through with her M.G.M. contract except for one film for which she was to get $100,000." That of course was to be *Butterfield 8.* "She had already signed a contract with Twentieth Century-Fox for a million to do *Cleopatra* and was anxious to go and make it. She was doing her best to get out of her M.G.M. commitment, so she wouldn't have liked anything we wanted her to make."

She would fulfill her contract, all right—but not without rebellion. She began her barrage against *Butterfield 8* even before she started to work in it.

"The role they want me to play is little better than a prostitute," she said. "Doing this picture gripes the hell out of me. . . . It's too commercial, it's in bad taste. Everyone in it is crazy, mixed-up, sick.''

Another of Elizabeth's blasts centered on the script. It was "the most pornographic script I've ever read." Then she went on to tell how she thought the studio was treating her unfairly. "The lady is almost a prostitute. A sick nymphomaniac. The whole thing is so unpalatable I wouldn't do it for anything—under any conditions."

O'Hara's famous novella was based on the true story of Starr Faithful, a hooker found murdered in Long Beach in 1931. However, Starr Faithful becomes more than a hooker in the story; O'Hara makes her a fashionable Manhattan beauty who's part model and part call girl. She suicides when she mistakenly thinks that a married socialite she loves, played by Laurence Harvey, will not divorce his wife to marry her.

"I don't know to this day if she really hated *Butterfield 8* or if it was just her ploy," Berman admitted. "In any case, it was a long story before we forced her to do it. We told her quite clearly that she would never, never make *Cleopatra* until she finished with us."

Elizabeth was furious with the M.G.M. brass. "You'll be sorry! You can make me do it, but you can't make me act in it. I won't show up! I'll be late!"

Berman shrugged. He knew she was such a total professional that she would never allow herself to act in an unprofessional manner. "I'll take that chance."

He was right.

At one time when the two of them were in an
acrimonious debate about the story Berman finally
shouted her down: "Now look, I'm going to tell
you something. You're going to win the Academy
Award with this picture!"

Elizabeth roared with laughter at him. So did her
agent.

But Elizabeth knew she had to fulfill the com-
mitment. So now came the haggling. She wanted
her husband, Eddie Fisher, in the picture. It was
agreed. Shooting date was confirmed. There was a
technicians' strike in Hollywood. The picture
would be made completely in New York.

Fisher now started on a singing engagement at
the Desert Inn in Las Vegas. It was his first work in
a year. Then, in November, he was hired for an
engagement at the Empire Room in the Waldorf
Astoria Hotel in New York. When it developed
that the press was pretty unexcited about it, Elizabeth had Blackstone invite 72 celebrities to be her
guests for the occasion. No freeloads were allowed.
Tins of caviar and champagne and assorted
beverages were held for six reserved tables. The tab
came to $1,500 for the night.

This was New York where boorishness was the
order of the day. A party of fifteen at one of the
tables refused to vacate after the first show. The
management could not unseat the party, headed by
a Brooklyn dentist.

It was not Fisher who threw them out. It was
Elizabeth. Once a shy maidenly young lady, Elizabeth Taylor Hilton Wilding Todd Fisher was not
about to be crossed by an orthodontist out on the
town. She sashayed over to the table in question,
her diamonds glittering in the light. There was

some soft dialogue, and then the decibel count rose. Elizabeth's "Irish" temper surged; the dentist matched it in rudeness.

"Lady, we knew Eddie when he was just a waiter at Grossinger's, and our money is as good as yours!"

Elizabeth had learned from Todd what to do with people who mentioned money. Out came the checkbook, and she wrote a $500 check to the dentist.

"God damn it," she snapped. "There's your money. Now get your asses out of here."

She still had not completely conquered her tendency to four-letter words.

It worked.

Fisher opened that night for a two-week engagement. He was okay, but nothing exceptional. It was the last time he worked for a year and a half. But that by no means meant that he was idle.

It was to be the year of death, resurrection, and almost deification.

The shooting of *Butterfield 8* was fairly routine, in spite of the conditions under which its initial concept was hammered out. Elizabeth kept bad-mouthing the picture and everything it stood for in public, and she dutifully reported to the set every day and did the part with the true craftsmanship and professionalism that were always hers.

"She did give us a little trouble here and there," Berman admitted. "But it was no more than she has given everybody on all her pictures: A little late once in a while. A little sick once in a while. Didn't like the clothes. Insisted on changing this and that."

Berman was noncommittal about Fisher's part in

the picture. He recalled that the singer got a couple writers to build up his part in the script. The male star of the picture was Laurence Harvey, playing Weston Liggett, the socialite with whom Elizabeth is in love. By the time the writers got the script in hand, Fisher's part, that of a male confidant, was as big as Harvey's.

"One day Liz and Eddie called me to come down to their hotel rooms," Berman said. "They handed me this batch of papers."

"Now this is something we would like to do," Elizabeth told him, eyeing him steadily.

Berman looked at the pile. He knew what it was. He picked up the script and walked over to the nearest wastebasket.

Berman: "She came flying out of that couch with her nails ready to scratch my eyes out! Spitting and hissing."

He tried to cool her down. "I won't read it. I'm not interested in any rewrites."

Fisher didn't get any added lines, and it was just as well. By most standards, he was stiff and flat in the role.

In spite of her stated determination to sabotage the picture, Elizabeth Taylor was the picture's most resounding success. "The picture's major asset is Miss Taylor, who makes what is becoming her annual bid for an Oscar," said *Variety*. "While the intensity and range of feeling that marked several of her more recent endeavors is slightly reduced in this effort, it is nonetheless a torrid, stinging overall portrayal with one or two brilliantly executed passages within . . . Eddie Fisher cannot unbend and get any warmth into his role."

"Elizabeth Taylor, who has a crackling effect on the screen, would dress up a rag-picker's shack," said Paul V. Beckley in the *New York Herald Tribune*. But Hollis Alpert in the *Saturday Review* hated it. "Miss Taylor obviously tries very hard to get a tragic quality into the girl—Lord, how she tries!—but not even acting can help this script."

But *Cue*'s Jesse Zunser disagreed: "With Elizabeth Taylor in the leading role giving the finest performance of her career, *Butterfield 8* shines with an insight into character in an honesty in story development not frequently met with in Hollywood dramas that so often glamorize the free-wheeling girls-about-town who refuse to face what they are because they accept, gifts, instead of money, for services too freely given."

It was to be three years before Elizabeth appeared on the screen again—and much would happen to her, to the next picture she was to make, and to all her close personal friends before then.

Cleopatra was to start shooting in London in September. The Fishers took a cruise in the Greek Islands before arriving in England. There they moved into a penthouse suite at the Dorchester Hotel. That was part of her deal with Fox. So were these incredible clauses:

- $1,000,000 for the job
- 10 percent of the picture's gross earnings
- $50,000 a week for overtime
- $3,000 a week living allowance
- round-trip transportation for Elizabeth and all their children to London or wherever
- all-expenses-paid round-trip for Kurt Frings (agent) per location

• two penthouses at the Dorchester in London
• use of a Silver Cloud Rolls-Royce and driver
• use of Todd-AO rather than Cinemascope (so she could get royalties)
• 16 millimeter print of the film

Now began the series of disasters that made *Cleopatra* one of the most doomed and accursed motion pictures ever to be made.

A little background on the picture:

The concept of *Cleopatra* had originally been born in the mind of Walter Wanger. When he mentioned *Cleopatra* to Skouras, the studio head told him to remake the old 1917 Theda Bara version. Wanger had bigger ideas. He wanted to get away from both that and the De Mille version made in 1934 with Claudette Colbert. He wanted a more modern approach: a combination of *Caesar and Cleopatra* and *Antony and Cleopatra*—the real life of the queen.

Wanger wanted Elizabeth Taylor from the start. He also wanted Laurence Olivier and Richard Burton. Burton was a Shakespearean actor who had been doing well not only on the stage but in films, too. Again, the Fox moguls wanted Cary Grant and Burt Lancaster. Or, for Caesar, John Gielgud, Yul Brynner, or Curt Jurgens; for Antony, Kirk Douglas, Marlon Brando, Stephen Boyd, Anthony Franciosa, Jason Robards, or Richard Basehart.

They finally settled for Stephen Boyd as Antony, and British actor Peter Finch as Caesar. Rouben Mamoulian, a Russian-born director, was assigned the picture. Several versions of the script were being prepared by various writers.

Shooting would be done at Pinewood Studios in England. Already, by September, 1961, $600,000 had been spent in building ancient Alexandria on eight and a half acres of studio land.

When shooting began on September 20, Elizabeth had a virus and fever which kept her temperature hovering around 100 degrees. The virus lasted for a full month. She could not work. Shooting started and leapfrogged her, taking exterior scenes where no dialogue was needed.

The temperature was forty-five degrees the first day, with only two minutes twenty seconds of sunshine. A heavy fog swirled in later on. A hundred extras got lost in it. Skouras wanted to shut down production, but the insurance company holding the *Cleopatra* policy went berserk.

"It was sheer lunacy," recalled Mamoulian. "The insurance people were full of nervous chicken."

They kept calling him up. "Shoot some film, shoot anything, as long as you can keep the film going!"

And so Mamoulian did, through the mud and the rain and the fog. "It was stinking weather. On a good day, whenever a word was spoken, you could see the vapor coming from the actors' mouths. It was like a tobacco commercial." Several hundred extras stood around, waiting.

There was not one frame of film with Elizabeth in it.

By the end of October Fox had already dropped $2 million on the picture. Skouras didn't like Peter Finch as Caesar. Mamoulian hated working in England because it was too wintry to resemble Egypt.

The script was not really in any acceptable shape. Elizabeth could not yet work. The *London Daily Mail* stated that she was "too plump"—their euphemism for fat. She sued them for a substantial sum, which she got.

On October 31, Elizabeth's virus had turned into influenza, and she was ordered into London Clinic. On November 2 she was diagnosed as having Malta fever, but then on November 10, it turned out that her trouble stemmed from an abscessed tooth, which was taken out. She was now ready to go to work.

Then, on November 14, she was taken out of the Dorchester on a stretcher, moaning and holding her head. This time her ailment was diagnosed as meningitis, an irritation of the spinal cord or brain. That was enough. Wanger arrived on the set four days later at Pinewood and announced that production was shutting down to resume on January 3.

The Fishers went to Paris on vacation, then flew to Palm Springs, and finally returned for the resumption of *Cleopatra*. On December 28, Elizabeth was in Makeup and Wardrobe. Mamoulian got the sequence in which Cleopatra appears before Caesar rolled up in the rug. When Elizabeth and Finch tried to do the dinner scene, they pronounced the script unplayable.

Nunnally Johnson was drafted to work on the script. Word was sent to Paddy Chayefsky to see if he was available. A total of $7 million dollars was gone already, and there was nothing on film that could be used—and still no workable script! Mamoulian threw in the towel on January 18. He was done. Elizabeth pleaded for her own release.

The Fishers flew to Munich February 13 for the Pre-Lenten Carnival. Three days later, Fisher was operated on for appendicitis at the London Clinic. Elizabeth was so worried about him that she caught the Asian flu. Fisher's appendectomy was taken care of, but her case of flu hung on. On March 4, she lapsed into unconsciousness and her face began turning blue and her fingernails black. Fisher was by her side. From a nearby suite at the Dorchester where he was attending a wedding reception, Dr. J. Middleton Price, one of London's most distinguished physicians, was summoned. He could see that she was slowly suffocating from lung congestion.

"I read later she had been given an hour to live," Price replied. "I'd say it was worse; she didn't have fifteen minutes."

Price told Fisher that he would have to perform an emergency operation on her throat so he could insert a tube to introduce oxygen into her lungs. The incision would leave a scar. Fisher told him to go ahead. Once the plastic tube was in place, pure oxygen was pumped into her lungs from an oxygen tank.

Price told Fisher that she would have to be moved to London Clinic where a tracheotomy would be performed. It was risky even moving her, but it had to be done. At the London Clinic, a team of surgeons working under Dr. Terence Cawthorne completed the tracheotomy and hooked up the plastic tube to a respirator. Her temperature began to fall and her breathing came more easily. But she was still unconscious.

She was then attached to a Barnet Ventilator, a portable electronic lung that measures the breathing electronically and strengthens and deepens it as needed. Her illness was soon diagnosed as acute staphylococcus pneumonia, which is often fatal. Along with the pneumonia, she was found to be suffering from anemia. Blood transfusions, intravenous feedings and doses of antibiotics were given her through an incision in her ankle.

But there was still no effective control. It also developed that she was allergic to some of the antibiotics that were necessary to her life.

Fisher telephoned Blackstone in New York. "She's allergic to the drugs they're giving her. There's one kind of serum that will help. Can you get it?" He named it.

Blackstone called Jacobson. The medicine was staphylococcal bacteriophage lysate. Jacobson procured it, gave it to Blackstone, and Blackstone flew to London to deliver it to London Clinic.

Huge crowds were now standing around outside the hospital. Thousands of letters were delivered every day. The new drug helped, and on March 10, Elizabeth Taylor was out of danger. She had made, according to the hospital, a "very rare recovery."

Elizabeth recalled her encounter with death as "terrifying." She thought at least four times that she was dead. "Four times after the initial time, I stopped breathing," she said. "When I came to that last time, it was like being given sight, hearing, touch, sense of color. Like I was, I don't know, twenty-nine years old, but had just come out of my own womb. I knew that I wanted more in my life than what I had."

Looking back at that moment—her death and resurrection—Elizabeth said later that her own life had a turning point in her illness in London. "I had been living ever since Mike's death with something deeply desperate within me. I was hoping to be happy, pretending to be happy. But I was in this indulgent lethargy, being consumed by self-pity instead of being grateful and glad over how lucky I was."

Later, she discussed how it felt to think she was dying.

"Dying, as I remember it, is many things—but most of all, it is wanting to live. Throughout many critical hours in the operating theater, it was as if every nerve, every muscle, as if my whole physical being were being strained to the last ounce of my strength, to the last gasp of my breath.

"Gradually and inevitably that last ounce was drawn, and there was no more breath. I remember I had focused desperately on the hospital light hanging directly above me. . . . Slowly it faded and dimmed, like a well-done theatrical effect, to blackness. I have never known, nor do I think there can be, a greater loneliness.

"Then it happened.

"First there was an awareness of hands. . . . Then the voices from a great distance at first, but ever so slowly growing louder. . . . I was no longer alone.

"I coughed, I moved, I breathed, and I looked. The hanging lamp—the most beautiful light my world has ever known—began faintly to glow again."

Even so close to death she was always irrepressibly Elizabeth Taylor. She was visited in her hospital room by Truman Capote who was visiting London. He brought her books to read.

She was, he said, whiter than the bedsheets, but lively even after that massive ordeal. And she was able to clown it up for him by showing him the wound in her throat that was stoppered with a small rubber plug.

"If I pull this out my voice disappears," she told him, and pulled it. Her voice did disappear. She giggled silently. Capote could not even hear her laughter until she reinserted the plug—an effect that unnerved him.

"It was like riding on a rough ocean," she told him, describing the ordeal. "Then slipping over the edge of the horizon. With the roar of the ocean in my head. Which I suppose was really the noise of my trying to breathe."

To recover his self-possession, Capote asked her the obvious question: if she had been afraid.

"I wasn't," she said. "I didn't have time to be. I was too busy fighting. I didn't want to go over that horizon. And I never will. I'm not the type."

The reaction of the rest of the world to her recovery was one of relief and then of great excitement. Her encounter with death aroused a tremendous wave of sympathy. By the time she was on the road to recovery, the public that had been booing and hissing her everywhere she went was once more her willing slave.

The Fishers flew to Los Angeles where Elizabeth checked into her suite at the Beverly Hills Hotel to convalesce. The effect of her narrow escape with death had transformed her husband from a loving spouse to a devoted attendant on twenty-four-hour service.

Fisher submerged his own personality in order to serve Elizabeth totally. As her closest servant he became a kind of "Mr. Elizabeth Taylor." But ever since their residence at the Dorchester the preceding fall, he had been snidely dubbed "The Busboy" by Elizabeth's associates.

Even friends of Fisher began saying that he was the prime example of a man who had grown up to mature into a little boy. Elizabeth and others thought that the reason for this subordinate behavior was the fact that Debbie Reynolds had cleaned him out financially in the divorce settlement.

"Debbie Reynolds—if you'll pardon the expression—got it all," Elizabeth said on more than one occasion.

By April 18, she was well enough to attend the Academy Awards ceremony. Her leg was still bothering her. Fisher walked along beside her, helping her walk. Elizabeth Taylor had been nominated for the Best Actress Award for her part in *Butterfield 8*—exactly as Pandro S. Berman had prophesied—and it was her fourth nomination.

When she learned that she had won, she put her hands up to her face and looked at her husband. Fisher helped her walk up to the stage to get the award. Elizabeth Taylor knew that the Oscar had been given her not for the role she had played but as a kind of apology for the way the Academy had treated her two years before when she was up for her part in *Cat*—and *really* deserved it.

She was not alone in her belief. "I was beaten by a tracheotomy," nominee Shirley MacLaine remarked after it was all over. *Life* magazine was even more pungent: "Liz nearly had to die to wrest the prize from her reluctant peers."

In July, Fisher made his first singing appearance since the Waldorf-Astoria in 1959. A charity performance with funds going to Eddie Cantor's Surprise Lake Camp, the affair was held at the Cocoanut Grove in the Ambassador Hotel on Wilshire Boulevard in Los Angeles.

Fisher was very nervous. The affair was a disaster. Frank Sinatra and the Rat Pack were on hand, and upstaged him mercilessly, hardly allowing him to finish his numbers.

Meanwhile, *Cleopatra* was being revived, with a brand new script, and with Joseph L. Mankiewicz as director rather than Mamoulian. Rome had been selected as the site of the shooting.

In September, Elizabeth Taylor and Eddie Fisher said goodbye to their friends in Hollywood and set out for Rome. *Cleopatra* would change their lives and the lives of everybody around them.

CHAPTER TEN
Antony of Pontfhydyfen

Cleopatra II was quite a different property from *Cleopatra* I, if we separate the two and label the Pinewood Studios version as *I* and the Cinecittà Studios version as *II*. Except for the role of Cleopatra, all the actors playing the principals were different, as was the director.

Mamoulian, as related, had quit in a combination of pique, disgust, and despair—plus a bit of a shove from Spyros P. Skouras. Joseph L. Mankiewicz, as related, had then been assigned director in his place. But he was not only to be director; he was to be script-writer as well.

In fact, by the time Mankiewicz was aboard, the entire story was shaping up quite differently from the original concept. Mankiewicz wanted to stick more closely to the original historical material as it appeared in Plutarch, Suetonius, and Appian. And he wanted to concentrate on the psychological implications and character relationships rather than the pomp and circumstance of ancient royalty.

In the Mankiewicz concept, the story becomes a

struggle between Caesar and his protégé, Mark Antony, with Mark Antony spending his life trying to surpass the accomplishments of his idol, and succeeding only in his conquest of Cleopatra. This in turn becomes his undoing, the conqueror being vanquished ultimately by the conquered. The point of view becomes essentially a modern treatment of the ancient theme, making Cleopatra the enticement and the emasculator rather than the allmighty vamp and beauty of cinematic tradition.

As for the actors, Peter Finch was out as Julius Caesar, and Rex Harrison was in. Stephen Boyd was out and Wanger's original second choice, Richard Burton, was in for Mark Antony. Burton had been playing King Arthur in *Camelot* on Broadway during *Cleopatra* I.

Harrison was a real find for Wanger. He signed because Mankiewicz was directing. And Wanger was lucky again. He got Burton—but not without a hassle.

Twentieth-Century Fox was going through a tremendous upheaval, a power struggle that was cracking apart the studio's behemoth structure. Skouras, the Greek immigrant who spoke fractured English, still didn't like Burton. His reasoning was that no American audience could understand Burton's English diction. "Like I can't understand you?" Burton shot back.

Wanger and Mankiewicz finally persuaded Skouras to hire Burton. Nobody knew it at the time, but Burton was to be one half of the international liaison known through popular history as *le scandale;* Elizabeth was to be the other half.

Richard Burton came into the world as Richard

Walter Jenkins, the twelfth of thirteen children born to a hard-drinking miner and a former barmaid in the black hills of South Wales, where unpronounceable names are standard roadmap fare. The town of his birth was Pontfhydyfen, a tiny coal-mining hamlet lying on two hills by the narrow Afan River as it runs down to Swansea Bay.

Young Jenkins came from a family of hard-drinking, hard-living, hard-hitting Welshmen, half-mad, half-sober, and sometimes half-witted. His grandfather met his end in a typical Welsh manner: confined to a wheelchair with both legs ruined in a mine accident, he got himself stoned in a local pub and ran the wheelchair down the hill pretending to be a jockey yelling, "Coom on, Black Sambo!" when he smashed into a stone wall and killed himself.

His father likewise was a toper of the first order who vanished once for three weeks before reappearing, gray-faced and glassy-eyed, at the kitchen door, holding in his hand a frayed rope, at the end of which staggered a mangy skeletal greyhound named Paris, the saddiest animal ever seen. "Boys," gasped the old sot, "our troubles are over!"

Richard weighed twelve pounds at birth; his father considered that fateful and downed twelve whiskies with a like number of beer chasers. When his mother died two years later after delivering her thirteenth child, Richard was sent to live with his sister. He escaped the mines because of a flair for letters, although he was not a particularly good student.

Deep depression hit Wales and his sister's hus-

band fell sick; Richard was without a home. Philip
Burton, a drama instructor interested in teaching
Richard Shakespeare, volunteered to care for him;
he legally adopted him. Richard took his name.

During World War II he was enlisted in the
R.A.F., and for one six-month period was sent to
Oxford for part of his service training. There a
Shakespearean scholar heard him reciting
Shakespeare and recommended he try the theater.

Emlyn Williams gave him his start after the war
had ended. His forte was Shakespeare, but he developed into a rugged, powerful, virile and almost
overpowering actor. The hulking strength, com-
bined with the soaring Shakespearean diction, riv-
eted everyone who saw him. It was not the beauty
of the body but the absolute mass of it that com-
manded attention.

Sir John Gielgud, Burton's stage idol, once was
describing another actor to Burton: "He's built like
a peasant. Just like you, Richard."

"Stripped, I'm a monster," Burton admitted.
"I've got a body like an abandoned dressing room.
When I took my clothes off to appear in bathing
trunks [once], strong men laughed and strangers
kissed each other."

Truman Capote once described him as "a light-
eyed man with a lilting, Welsh-valley voice, and an
acne-rough complexion you could scratch a match
on." Burton had a Welshman's sense of humor and
an irrepressible predisposition to the ribald.

In his early days, he loved to practice speech delivery in the men's lavatory, letting his voice ring
out in the confined space and watching the faces of
visitors as he spoke Macbeth's lines:

Is this a dagger which I see before me,
The handle toward my hand? Come, let me clutch
thee. . . .

Like many Welshmen, Burton suffered from that ancient curse of the Celts—the black melancholy—that came over him with a kind of unpredictable regularity. The Welsh word for the phenomenon is *hiraeth,* meaning, literally, "a longing for unnamable things." Traditionally, the Welshman with sensitivity suffers periods of semicomas or blackouts of depression, worrying themselves toward self-destruction.

Later on, when he had met, romanced, and married Elizabeth Taylor, she described the phenomenon as Burton's "Welsh hour," and called it a "whirlpool of black molasses, carrying them down, down, down."

It was something, she admitted, that one had to put up with when loving a Welshman.

Emlyn Williams introduced Burton to Sybil Williams, who was no relation of his. Sybil, like Richard, came from a Welsh mining village. They were married in 1951 in a simple and quiet ceremony, after which Mrs. Burton had to rush out to appear in a matinee performance of *Harvey* and Richard tuned in the radio to the Scotland-Wales Championship Rugby Match.

Sybil appeared several times in dramas with Richard. When they played together at Stratford, some of her reviews were better than his.

"That was when I told her, 'Dear, the time has come for you to pack it in!' " Burton said. And so she did. She bore him two daughters, Kate and Jessica.

Burton played in Christopher Fry's play *The Lady's Not for Burning,* made several undistinguished British movies—undistinguished with the exception of *Room at the Top*—and finally was called to Hollywood to make *My Cousin Rachel* with Olivia de Havilland.

Although he preferred his British friends to Americans generally, he did strike up a true friendship with Humphrey Bogart. They were two of a kind—ruggedly individual, professional to the core, and contemptuous of fraud. One night at a party the two of them, heavily sedated with booze, ran into a dignified guest who said that he had been raised by an English nanny.

"Did you fuck her?" Bogart asked.

No answer from the startled gentleman. Burton broke in: "Unless you did, you can't possibly lay claim to being a proper member of the bloody ruling class!"

Bogart and Burton walked off laughing. Bogart then asked a gray-haired lady: "I've got to take a leak—can you direct me to the men's room?"

Burton winked. "The real truth is that we are *that way* about each other and we need privacy!"

Burton's female conquests were legion. Sybil understood. She put up with his philandering because she knew he would never leave her. It was all part of the Welsh psyche she understood so well. But at times even her wifely tolerance was tested to the extreme.

The Burtons shared quarters with the Stewart Grangers in Los Angeles. Then Burton was assigned to a role opposite Jean Simmons—Mrs. Stewart Granger—in *The Robe.* Shortly after the picture was made, the Burtons and Grangers were celebrating New Year's at a party. When the bells tolled in the new year, Burton kissed Simmons rather than Sybil, who was waiting patiently, as it were, in the wings. She expected him to be with her at least for this sentimental moment.

When it was over, she strode purposefully to the center of the room, slapped Burton's face, and left the party. Subsequently, the Burtons moved out of the Grangers' house and rented a cottage elsewhere.

The pictures Burton made in Hollywood were all right, but nothing exceptional. One, *Bramble Bush*, was an absolute dog; neither Burton nor Angie Dickinson could save it. Burton was actually better on stage than on film.

About this time Alan K. Lerner and Frederick Loewe had just finished a new musical called *Jennie Kissed Me,* based on T. H. White's version of the King Arthur legend, *The Once and Future King*. Lerner and Loewe had seen Burton playing Shakespeare, and knew they wanted him. Retitled *Camelot,* the musical was the best thing Burton was to do up to that time in the States.

When *Cleopatra* II was ready for shooting, Burton had played on Broadway for a year, and felt that all the challenge was gone and the role was becoming routine. He needed something new. He gladly signed with Fox for the part of Antony.

Besides, he was a good friend of Rex Harrison's, and he knew many in the cast, including Roddy McDowall, who had worked with him in *Camelot*. With Sybil and the children, he flew to Rome and settled down in the villa on the Appian Way where

McDowall was living.

The shooting schedule was more or less in sequence; that meant that Rex Harrison's Caesar would be before the cameras for about half of the schedule, with Burton's Antony before the cameras for the second half. Burton loafed around during the first weeks and months, sometimes visiting the set, but more frequently reading and writing and doing what he wanted to do. Even a little drinking.

Meanwhile, the Fisher family moved into a fourteen-room mansion called the Villa Pappa on the Appian Way in Rome. Elizabeth now had a huge garden surrounding a mansion, and a swimming pool and tennis court outside. For the children, of course.

The Fisher entourage was formidable: besides Elizabeth Taylor and Eddie Fisher—now almost completely reincarnated into "The Busboy"—there were the three children, Michael Wilding Jr., Christopher Wilding, and Liza Todd; Elizabeth's Hollywood physician, Dr. Rexford Kennamar; and servants to the number of sixteen, including a children's governess, a general handyman, a butler, three male and four female servants, a cook and kitchen helper, a laundress, and a woman who did the pressing and ironing, a chauffeur for Elizabeth's Cadillac and a chauffeur for "The Busboy's" Rolls-Royce.

Shooting started out fairly uneventfully. Elizabeth spent most of her first weeks working with Rex Harrison. Harrison, like Elizabeth, was the total film professional—but he was a human being underneath, too. His contract provided for a chauffeur-driven Cadillac from the Via Antiqua, where he was living, to the studio. One morning he went out to find the chauffeur sitting in a Mercedes-Benz. Harrison wondered aloud where the Caddy was.

"They say it's too expensive," the chauffeur said.

Harrison climbed in, doing a slow burn. On the set he demanded to see "the money man." The production manager duly appeared.

"Where's my Cadillac?" Harrison thundered.

"We felt perhaps you wouldn't mind a Mercedes —it's a little cheaper."

Harrison went through the ceiling. "I want my Cadillac and I want it now!" he shouted. "I will *not* appear on the set until my Cadillac is back." He turned and glanced at Elizabeth who was waiting to do the same. "And what's more, I understand that Elizabeth Taylor's chauffeur is paid far more than my chauffeur. I insist that my chauffeur get the same pay as Elizabeth Taylor's chauffeur. Why the hell should Elizabeth Taylor's chauffeur get more than my chauffeur *just because she's got a bigger chest?*"

Things were finally settled to Harrison's satisfaction, and work proceeded. The huge cast of people included Roddy McDowall, Hume Cronyn, Pamela Brown, and even Carroll O'Connor, long before he struck it rich as Archie Bunker in *All in the Family* on television.

Elizabeth had an entire five-room building as a dressing room—an office for The Busboy, a relaxation and receiving salon for visitors, a room devoted to Elizabeth's wigs, a dressing room, a makeup room, and a bath and shower.

During the first months of filming, Elizabeth

rarely saw Burton at all. She had met him, years before, at Stewart Granger's in Los Angeles. She remembered him as a man who was "rather full of himself." But she was nevertheless in awe of his reputation as a Shakespearean actor. In fact, she envied his theatrical background; he was a "genuine actor," whereas she was only a "movie actor."

Burton was skeptical about McDowall's fascination with Elizabeth Taylor. He kept needling him, but McDowall kept telling him how good she was. Burton had never seen any of her movies. But he watched her surreptitiously on the set as she worked with Harrison and he was not impressed. He dismissed her as a "fat little tart."

For some time now the Fishers had been thinking of adopting a child. Elizabeth had been warned not to have any more children. With the help of Kurt Frings, her agent at the time, she had finally located a little girl in Germany. At the age of nine months, Maria had been found in a laundry basket on top of two pillows suffering from extreme malnutrition. Covered with abscesses, she was discovered to have a crippled hip. Now a year old, she was undergoing a series of operations at a Munich clinic to correct the defect.

Finally, on January 15, the adoption papers went through. The Fishers proudly and happily announced the addition to their family.

By now the Burtons and the Fishers had been introduced to each other, formally as well as informally. They were together at a dinner dance given by the Kirk Douglases, and the Fishers had visited the set to watch Burton at work with Harrison. On New Year's Eve the Burtons threw a party, to which the Fishers were invited as guests of honor. The two couples occasionally nightclubbed together on Rome's steamy Via Veneto.

Exactly one week after Maria's adoption, Elizabeth Taylor and Richard Burton were scheduled to play their first scene together before the cameras. And, almost immediately, sparks began to fly. Burton had been out celebrating the night before, and arrived at the set hung over and shaken.

"He was kind of quivering from head to foot," Elizabeth said. She helped him steady his hand enough to gulp down black coffee. Then, later, when he blew one of his lines, she realized he was human. "My heart just went out to him."

It was that quick and that decisive. Elizabeth and Burton weren't just playing Cleopatra and Antony, they were *living* the story. Wanger watched them doing their scene together and said, "You could almost feel the electricity between Liz and Burton."

Now the Fishers began to appear more and more on the town with the Burtons. There was little gossip at first. With Fisher urging Elizabeth to get home and to bed, and Burton urging Elizabeth to stay a little longer, she was torn—but knew which way to turn. Not in her husband's direction.

Mankiewicz saw what was happening. He and Wanger began to worry. "I've been sitting on a volcano all alone for too long," he told Wanger. "I want to give you some facts you ought to know. Liz and Burton are not just *playing* Antony and Cleopatra."

Since Mike Todd's death, Elizabeth had worn his wedding ring, which, twisted and charred, had been removed from the wreck in New Mexico. During shooting scenes she pinned it to her under-clothes. Now the ring vanished from sight; it was packed away with her things.

Elizabeth had turned from her husband to Burton. But with the new arrival of her adopted daughter Maria from Germany, she did not want to make the switch obvious to the public. A scandal of a break-up and an affair with Burton might ruin the adoption proceedings.

By the end of January, almost everyone connected with *Cleopatra* was aware of what was happening between the two stars. Actually, the press was alerted to the fact, but the press was too cynical to bite. The media generally assumed that such a "love affair" was strictly an item dreamed up by the publicity mills. Nobody bit on that kind of stuff anymore.

Burton did an interview for the *London Sunday Express*. "Liz is absolutely marvelous," he told Roderick Mann. "They did a breathtaking shot of her the other day lying absolutely nude on a day bed. That ought to be good for around $20 million on its own. I must say Liz fascinates me. What is it about her, I wonder, that makes her so good? Off the screen she's just a nice, charming girl. But on the screen, she is absolutely compelling. She looks at you with those eyes and your blood churns, I tell you."

That clinched it. The "affair" was strictly publicity.

In reality, the marriage between Elizabeth Taylor and Eddie Fisher was over—but Fisher didn't know it yet. In late January Elizabeth ordered the set closed to visitors, including her husband. She did not want to let him see how things were between her and Burton. By now Elizabeth was relaxing her hold on her husband. Fisher felt relieved; she wasn't clinging to him quite so much.

Fisher decided that at last Elizabeth was recovering from the effect of Mike Todd's death. It was time, he decided, for him to pursue his own sagging career. He contacted Blackstone and then flew back to New York in February to arrange some recording sessions with Blackstone and try to sign up a series of nightclub appearances.

Arrivederci, Eduardo!

That night suddenly Elizabeth Taylor and Richard Burton appeared out in the open in Rome, dining and dancing until the wee hours of the morning.

The affair which had been blazing in the background, the affair which Wanger and Mankiewicz were cognizant of and feared with every atom of their being, the affair which Burton himself later dubbed with typical boulevardier flair "*Le Scandale,*" the affair between Welsh coalminer's son and an American art dealer's daughter, was on.

CHAPTER ELEVEN
Le Scandale

First Eddie and Debbie—with Elizabeth coming between them.

Now Richard and Sybil—with Elizabeth coming between them?

There was a certain Greek inevitability about it, and had been, from the beginning. The beauty and femininity of Elizabeth; the power and virility of Burton. How could they avoid an earth-shattering collision?

For some reason, no one had thought the affair would happen. Not Sybil, who was counting on her husband's faithfulness without understanding the potency of Elizabeth Taylor's beauty. Not Eddie Fisher, who apparently did not understand that he was simply an interlude in Elizabeth Taylor's life between the high of Mike Todd and the summit of Richard Burton.

But by now everybody was in on the affair.

It was even in the *London Times*. If it was in the *Times*, it had to be true. Emlyn Williams, probably one of Burton's closest friends and confidants, flew into a tantrum when he learned the truth. Then he grabbed a jet for Rome, bursting in on Burton to give him a tongue-lashing for what he was doing to Sybil.

The two of them had a knock-down-drag-out shouting match. Ironically, it was interrupted by the appearance of Elizabeth, looking shining and innocent and as beautiful as ever.

Williams turned to Burton, snarling at him in disgust. "Look at her! She's just a third-rate chorus girl!"

Burton looked stunned. Then he burst out laughing.

When Williams returned to his wife in England to report the dialogue, she reacted with quick anger. "Emlyn! When you met me, *I* was a third-rate chorus girl!"

Philip Burton, closer to Burton even than Emlyn Williams—since he had given Burton his name—was outraged at his foster son. Sick in New York, he was unable to appear on the scene, or he would have.

Sybil Burton, used to her husband's philanderings, maintained her dignity through the first stormy days of *Le Scandale*. The night before Eddie Fisher had flown to New York, he had telephoned her, complaining that her husband was having an affair with Elizabeth—an affair that might break up the Fisher marriage.

That was too much, being a confidante of a husband cuckolded by *her* husband. She challenged Burton the next morning. Burton sulked.

On the set Wanger approached Burton. He too had heard from Fisher. He warned Burton that his dalliance could wreck the picture, could hurt too many people, could even bring down Twentieth-Century Fox.

Burton mulled it over. To him, the affair was a simple and casual liaison that would be over when the picture was in the can. But he knew he was being scorched by the intensity of it already. He wondered if it could be ended with a simple "*Ciao, bébé. Buona fortuna!*"

News came from New York that ailing Philip Burton was in a very bad way. Sybil promised to fly over to see him. Burton realized his foster father's illness might be a result of *Le Scandale*. Putting Sybil on the jet for the States, he mulled it over and that afternoon called Wanger. The two of them talked some more, and Burton wound up promising him that he would break it off. With Sybil out of the way, he could have one last evening with Elizabeth. It would be the best way to cool it with her. Besides that, it would be a good clean break. Burton had finished work in *The Longest Day* just before coming to Rome; now there were retakes to be made. He was scheduled to fly to France the next day.

They were alone together when Burton told her that he had finally made up his mind. Their relationship, he said, was endangering not only his marriage, but his relationship with his close associates. But he was not going to leave Sybil, no matter what happened. Nothing—but nothing—was going to break up what he and his wife had together. And so it would be impossible for this thing between them to go on.

Elizabeth listened in stunned silence. She knew

Burton was lying to himself as well as to her. She
knew what she felt, and she knew what he really
felt. He was trying to fool himself. She reacted with
calm at first, but she told him exactly what she
thought. Then, as she continued, and Burton said
nothing, she burst into tears and became almost
hysterical.

Alarmed, Burton took her to the Villa Pappa
and left her there. She was sobbing and screaming
at him. When he closed the glass door behind him
and walked off into the night, she tried to crash
through it to chase after him. She was restrained by
Dick Hanley. He finally got her to bed.

Hanley called Wanger later, explaining that Elizabeth would not be able to work on the set next
day.

Wanger was worried. He hurried over to the Villa Pappa and learned that his star was in bed and
being treated by a physician. Later Elizabeth appeared briefly and talked to him.

"I feel dreadful," she confessed. "Sybil is such a
wonderful woman." It was a cryptic remark, and in
the middle of the conversation, Elizabeth drifted
upstairs to rest. Wanger and Hanley were joined by
Roddy McDowall and Elizabeth's hairdresser. Before leaving, Wanger went up to see how she was
feeling. She had taken some pills and was sleepy.

Later one of the servants took sandwiches and
milk upstairs and saw that she was in a deep deep
sleep. Too deep.

"Miss Taylor's taken pills!" called the servant.

Someone set for the ambulance. When Elizabeth
reached Salvator Mundi Hospital, the *paparazzi*
were waiting with their cameras and flashbulbs.
"Liz Poisoned in Rome!" cried the headlines. That

was the cover story—something about "a bad bowl of chili." Chili in Rome? Like pizza in Acapulco. Wanger mentioned "bad beef." Garbled stories came out: a nervous breakdown, a Seconal overdose, an attempted suicide. Sybil's departure for New York was rumored to be a trip to file divorce proceedings.

Fisher flew back to Rome looking beat to the socks. When he finally got in to see her and came out, the *paparazzi* were told: "I've got nothing to say."

Elizabeth's plight brought Burton flying back from Paris. He saw her and then sat down with his publicity agent, Chris Hofer.

"For the past several days uncontrolled rumors have been growing about Elizabeth and myself," the statement said. "Statements attributed to me have been distorted out of proportion, and a series of coincidences has lent plausibility to a situation which has become damaging to Elizabeth. Mr. Fisher, who has business interests of his own, merely went out of town to attend to them for a few days. My foster-father, Philip Burton, has been quite ill in New York, and my wife, Sybil, flew there to be with him for a time, since my schedule does not permit me to be there. He is very dear to both of us. Elizabeth and I have been close friends for over twelve years. I have known her since she was a child star and would certainly never do anything to hurt her personally or professionally. In answer to these rumors, my normal inclination would be simply to say 'No comment,' but I feel that in this case things should be explained to protect Elizabeth."

The Fox brass blew its top when it read the

statement. The studio claimed that the statement was made without Burton's knowledge. Elizabeth then made a statement: the whole business was "nonsense." Fisher rallied with Elizabeth, and they presented a happy front to the world.

Fox said: "Mrs. Burton is in Rome with her husband now. All this is typical *Dolce Vita* set rumor. Whenever a good-looking man and a beautiful girl play a love scene everyone here starts trying to make something out of it."

Next day Fox leaned on Burton. Burton claimed that he had never issued nor authorized the denial of a romance that he now said had never existed. "I have always believed that professional publicity should be kept as far as possible from one's personal life. Now, more than ever before, I believe my reasoning is justified." He said all rumors of a romance were "bloody nonsense."

Hofer was left with his foot in his mouth. He issued this statement: "If Richard says he knew nothing about it, I have to go along with him. After all, I work for him."

Wanger observed that the whole incident had burnished Burton's image rather than tarnished it. In spite of the turmoil that swirled about him, he appeared on the set cocky, jaunty, and suave. Burton had been transformed overnight from a well-known star who was not really famous to that immeasurable commodity—a household word. The romance with Elizabeth was changing his life; had already changed it, unalterably.

Mankiewicz was the only one who acted with any kind of show biz élan. He planted a story in *Time* magazine that put a beard on Burton and diverted all the heat to himself. The beard, that time-honored scam of adding a third party in public to a secret twosome on the pretense that the beard—the third party—is really the lover, in his case was Mankiewicz. The story read:

"Burton, according to gossip, has made more than his mark as Antony. Taylor, according to gossip, is merely using the Burton rumors to shield the real truth: she is mad, mad, mad for her personable director, Joseph L. Mankiewicz, 53, who, however, is very busy shooting all day and scripting all night."

To prove that everything was eternal bliss in Rome, Fisher threw a big champagne bust for Elizabeth on her thirtieth birthday—February 27. The party was given at the Borgia Room of the Hostaria del Orso. An expensive diamond ring and an elaborate antique mirror were presented to her to prove to the press that everything was the same as ever.

Next day Fisher showed up on the set to find out what was going on. He saw. If there was nothing between them, what in the world was *this?* "They couldn't keep their eyes, not to mention their hands, off each other," he recalled later. Taking his life in his hands, Fisher approached Burton.

Burton got in the first blow. "I think you should know I'm in love with your girl."

"She's not my *girl.* She's my wife."

"I'm in love with her, so bugger off, Fisher!"

Fisher considered punching Burton in the nose. But if he did that, he would have the media on Burton's side. There were other ways to worry Burton, but Fisher never found the right solution. Perhaps. . . .

Blackstone was with him. He talked his client

into leaving Rome and returning to New York to get his career under way again. Then Blackstone telephoned Earl Wilson and gave him the story of the confrontation.

On March 3, Burton did not show up on the set until ten o'clock. He had been visiting the night before with a show girl from New York with whom he had liaisoned during his appearance in *Camelot*. He had appeared at his dressing room at seven a.m. that morning, with her in tow. What had kept him? What indeed.

Elizabeth took him on first. "You've kept us waiting."

"That's a switch," Burton snarled. "It's about time somebody kept *you* waiting for a change."

Harrison quickly came between them. "Let's rehearse, everyone," he said pleasantly.

The show girl hung around watching the acting for several days. Finally Wanger kicked her off the set and she left town.

On March 8 Louella Parsons published a story about the Burton-Taylor affair that virtually spelled out divorce. Skouras, worrying his head off at Fox, grabbed a plane with Otto Koegel, the studio's legal counsel, and arrived in Rome to "straighten things out."

Skouras blamed Wanger for hiring Burton; Burton was the cause of all the trouble. With absolutely no appreciation for the people nor the passions with which he was dealing, he sat down and wrote a letter to Burton, ordering him to clean up his private life.

His intention was to write a memo to Elizabeth too. Burton went totally berserk when his warning was delivered. Immediately he called Elizabeth and waved it at her. She flew to Wanger, storm flags flying, informing Wanger that if Skouras said a word to her, she would quit immediately.

Largely as a result of the column Louella Parsons had written, Sara and Francis Taylor arrived in Rome. Of all their sons-in-law, Fisher appealed to them the most. Fisher squired them around Rome, showing them the sights. He also filled them in on *Le Scandale*. This time it was Francis who acted.

He sat down with his daughter and gave her a tongue-lashing that thoroughly unnerved her. She was in tears, crying all night. She did not report to the set next day, but sent word that she could not make it.

Several days later, however, Sara and Francis were out on the town with Richard Burton! The *paparazzi* found them at Bulgari's, where they had gone to purchase a jewel that Elizabeth had previously suggested she wanted. Her father actually selected the emerald. There was, according to the story, a shopping procession of "parents, hairdresser, faggots, and other members of the court."

Things seemed to quiet down for a few days. On March 21, Fisher flew to New York for a recording session that Blackstone had set up for him. On the same day Sybil Burton and the two children flew to London. Blackstone did not take Fisher to the recording studio immediately but instead put him in Gracie Square Hospital in New York for a rest. Jacobson took charge of him, trying to provide the necessary injections to neutralize his anger and humiliation at the Burton-Taylor affair. News of his hospitalization leaked out. Erroneous news reports said he was in a "psychiatric ward," supposedly suffering from a nervous breakdown.

Finally, rested and looking fit, in plaid sport jacket and gray slacks, Fisher left the hospital and called a press conference on March 30, at the Hotel Pierre. His statement began: the reports of a break-up between him and Elizabeth Taylor were "preposterous, ridiculous, absolutely false."

"One thing is undeniable," he said. "I love Liz, and she loves me. The marriage is fine. Just fine. Even before I married, the wiseacres were saying it would never last. Well, it's lasted this long and it's going to last a lot longer. . . . The only romance between Elizabeth and Richard Burton is Mark Antony and Cleopatra."

Someone asked him if Elizabeth would deny rumors of an affair with Burton.

Fisher apparently was on some kind of high provided by Jacobson's pills. "I think she will—yes."

"Will you get her on the phone right now and ask her to deny the reports?" The noose was nicely fashioned, waiting for Fisher to stick his head through it.

"Yes, I will," Fisher said. The noose hung poised.

From the adjoining room Fisher telephoned Elizabeth in Rome. He told her he wanted her to explain to the media that there was no foundation for the stories.

"Well, Eddie," Elizabeth said, "I can't do that because there is some truth in the story. I just can't do that."

Fisher was stunned. "Wait a minute! What do

you mean, you won't do that?"

"I can't do that because it's true," Elizabeth explained patiently. "There *is* a foundation to the story."

"Thanks a lot!" snarled Fisher, and hung up. He was ashen-faced when he came before the assemblage of reporters. "You know you can ask a woman to do something, but she doesn't always do it."

"Liz Turns Down Eddie's Ocean Phone Call Love Plea," said the headlines next day.

A few hours after that denouement, Elizabeth and Burton were once again nightclubbing around Rome until dawn. They visited Bricktop's, and then Il Pipistrello (The Bat), arm in arm and smiling even at the inevitable *paparazzi*.

Soon the Munich orphanage where the Fishers had found Maria became concerned because of the publicity. The German Embassy in Rome told the press that it had been making inquiries into little Maria Fisher's welfare.

On April 12 an Open Letter in the Vatican City weekly, *L'Osservatore della Domenica*, was addressed to Elizabeth Taylor:

"Dear Madame: When some time ago, you said that your marriage (your fourth) would last for your whole life, there were some who shook their heads in a rather skeptical way. We, always willing to believe the best, kept our heads steadily on our shoulders and did not say a word. Then, when you reached the point of adopting a baby girl, as if to make more stable this marriage which had no natural children, for a moment we really believed that things had changed. But children—whether they

are natural or adopted—count little for illustrious
ladies like you when there is nothing for them to
hold together. It appears that you had the bad taste
to state: 'My marriage is dead and extra-dead!'
And what of the 'whole life' you had declared it
would last three years ago? Does your whole life
mean only three years? And if your marriage is
dead, then we must say, according to the Roman
usage, it was killed dead. The trouble is, my dear
lady, you are killing too many. . . ." And so on.

Elizabeth appeared with Burton at the Grand
Hotel that night where they had dinner. Then she
and he were off to meet Mike Nichols in a Via
Veneto nightclub. The streets were crowded with
people. "Home wrecker!" came the shouts. "Unfit
mother!"

Elizabeth broke down and sobbed uncon-
trollably. She rushed home in her car. Burton left
alone later, hounded by the *paparazzi*.

After the attack from the Vatican, Elizabeth and
Burton promised Wanger that they would stay out
of the papers. Sara and Francis were still in town,
and Elizabeth left the children with them on the
Easter weekend. She and Burton traveled 100 miles
north to Porto Santo Stefano, a posh seaside resort. They stayed five miles from the town in a se-
cluded hotel on a promontory overlooking the Tyr-
rhenian Sea.

When she showed up in Rome again she had a
black eye and a bruised nose. The *paparazzi*
sneaked pictures of her; the journalists speculated:
had she tried to kill herself in front of her lover?
Did Burton punch her in the eye?

Once again Elizabeth was hospitalized at

Salvator Mundi Hospital. The official explanation was that she had hurt her nose and eye when her driver had braked the car quickly on the way home.

The *paparazzi* continued to haunt her. She and Burton were sailing with friends of Burton's on a yacht just out of Naples. Elizabeth felt that she was being watched. Burton snorted and warned her not to imagine things. When Elizabeth asked one of the waiters to throw back a curtain separating the dining area and the ship's galley, they found a camera crew taking pictures of them behind the curtain.

On the set one day Elizabeth found a small camera hidden under an elaborate piled-up hairdo one of the extras was wearing. A *paparazzo* claiming to be a roof repairer hung down from the roof of the Villa Pappa and tried to take upside-down pictures through an open window in the bedroom.

Because of all the intrigue around the villa, Elizabeth and Burton chose to spend most of their time together at a hideaway one-room flat down on the seashore. It was a "crummy" place, according to Elizabeth. "We'd spend weekends there. I'd barbecue. There was a crummy old shower, and the sheets were always damp. We loved it—absolutely adored it."

On May 3, a burly, husky man in heavy dark glasses sauntered into the Grand Hotel in Rome, and was admitted to a room in which columnist Sheila Graham was staying. Burton took off his dark glasses and had a heart-to-heart chat with her. In effect, he told her that there "was no chance" of his divorcing his wife. Graham pointed out to Burton that his affair with Elizabeth had made him a great star. "What a shameful way to become a star," Burton responded.

On May 22, Iris Blitch, a member of the House of Representatives from Georgia, suggested that the U.S. Attorney General take measures to determine whether or not Elizabeth Taylor and Richard Burton might be ineligible for reentry into the United States on the grounds of undesirability.

On June 23 Elizabeth filmed one of the concluding scenes of *Cleopatra*—shots of the barge arriving at Tarsus. It was a stupendous scene, costing $500,000 to film.

More than a month later, on July 28, the last final shot of *Cleopatra* was taken in Rome. Within days, the sets were dismantled. The picture was in the can, after ten months of semi-hysteria.

Elizabeth Fisher and Richard Burton packed their bags and left in different directions.

Cleopatra II was finished.

And so were the Taylor-Fisher and the Williams-Burton marriages, although neither was concluded at that time.

CHAPTER TWELVE
Onward and Upward

Although the shooting of *Cleopatra* was done, the picture was in no way completed and ready for exhibition. Nor were the repercussions of the picture's making at all silenced in Hollywood. Largely because of its enormous cost—it was eventually estimated at probably $62 million, although exact figures are impossible to come by—there were a series of upheavals in the board room that resulted in the final expulsion of Spyros P. Skouras as studio head.

As he lay ill in the hospital from a prostrate condition in May 1962, the board took over. Wanger was fired in June. Thus the man who had actually conceived and engineered the picture from beginning to end was out, never to return.

Mankiewicz offered to resign, but was not allowed the opportunity. In the middle of the month he too was fired. By then the last of the shots had been made. There were 96 hours of film—a total of 120 miles of celluloid—in the Fox vaults.

Skouras was then ousted as head of the studio as

the internal drama continued. Darryl F. Zanuck was called back from retirement to oversee the rehabilitation of the company. One of the first problems that faced him was the wrapup of *Cleopatra*. For that he needed Mankiewicz. Mankiewicz returned and took it upon himself to assemble this elephantine creation.

Finally he got a workable rough cut out of the 96 hours—it lasted 26 hours! Then he pared that down to eight hours of film. Eight hours is a full working day for an ordinary moviegoer. Mankiewicz saw a way out: release *two* pictures, calling one *Caesar and Cleopatra* and the other *Antony and Cleopatra*. In retrospect, this seems today the most logical solution of all. However, 1962 was long before the television mini-series concept had been popularly accepted, and long before Hollywood's *Jaws I* and *Jaws II*.

Zanuck refused to appreciate the value of that: one of the pictures might make money, he thought, but the other certainly could not. He ordered Mankicwicz to pare the eight hours down to four. Then the picture could be released with an intermission.

The only way Mankiewicz could get the vast bulk of the picture down to four hours was to cut out most of Antony's part—where the script established his character and focused on his urge to surpass his mentor. As a result, in the finished film, Antony never develops but more or less emerges full-blown as a kind of disintegrating lout.

The corporate windup of the most expensive picture of all time had a kind of Katzenjammer–Keystone Cops flavor to it: Wanger sued Skouras, Zanuck, and Fox for more than $2.5 million, charging breach of contract; he settled for $100,000. Elizabeth eventually sued Fox for misrepresentation of the gross profits. Fox sued the Burtons (after Richard had married Elizabeth) for $50 million, claiming that their scandalous liaison had hurt the picture's chances for success.

After years of wrangling, the suits were all finally settled. Elizabeth told Andy Warhol once that it developed that what Fox wanted was Elizabeth's 10 percent of the gross. She refused to part with that. In the end the mess between the Burtons and Fox was concluded out of court, with the Burtons laughing all the way to the bank with a cool two and a half million.

But that was later.

When *Cleopatra* was released in 1963, it drew the reactions expected from the critics. The intellectuals loathed it, perhaps because of its very pageantry and success with the public. The moralists hated it because it represented in their minds the excesses of the Burton-Taylor affair.

The *New York Post*'s Archer Winsten wrote: "It pains one to reflect that the Liz Taylor, so brutally overmatched here, who started her career with the perfection of *National Velvet* nineteen years ago, is over the edge. *Cleopatra* proves an expensive way to demonstrate it."

Typically, *Time* mixed plaudits with putdowns. "As for Taylor, she does her dead-level best to portray the most woman in world's history. To look at, she is every inch 'a morsel for a monarch.' Indeed, her 50 gorgeous costumes are designed to suggest that she is a couple of morsels for a monarch. But the 'infinite variety' of the superb

Egyptian is beyond her, and when she plays Cleopatra as a political animal she screeches like a ward heeler's wife at a block party."

Judith Crist's comment in the *New York Herald Tribune* was predictable: "Out of royal regalia, en negligee or au naturel, she gives the impression that she is really carrying on in one of Miami Beach's more exotic resorts."

In the *New Republic* Stanley Kaufman saw her in a similar light. "Miss Taylor is a plump, young American matron in a number of Egyptian costumes and makeups. She needs do no more than walk around the throne room to turn Alexandria into Beverly Hills."

Bosley Crowther, in *The New York Times:* "Elizabeth Taylor's Cleopatra is a woman of force and dignity, fired by a fierce ambition to conquer and rule the world."

But *Monthly Film Bulletin,* through John Dyer, didn't like it at all: "Elizabeth Taylor, in the past an underrated actress, here proves herself vocally, emotionally and intellectually overparted to a disastrous degree. Her rages (the burning of the library at Alexandria, the news of Antony's marriage) are the merest petulance; her beauty and cunning shorn of mystery and complexity. But how can you take a Cleopatra seriously who plays with plastic barges in the bath?"

It was not a happy occasion for Elizabeth Taylor —even with all that money that came out of the project. But if she lost the critics during those two years of filming, The Queen at least gained a consort.

On her exit from Rome, Elizabeth took her four

children and went for a rest to the Chalet Ariel, a cottage she had bought in Gstaad, Switzerland. It was there that she made a final decision about her relationship with Burton. By now, of course, Fisher and she had agreed to separate, although she was in no hurry for a divorce; nor was Fisher. *Time* snidely suggested in its cleverly convoluted verbal style that "if she had divorced Fisher and Burton had gone back to his wife, Taylor would have lost ten-tenths of her pretty face!"

Not completely true. Max Lerner, who at one time was working on an authorized autobiography with her, said later that she was willing to risk everything to live with Burton without marriage. He refused, because the stakes were too steep for him to wager for only a semi-status.

At Gstaad, she wrote a long letter to Burton explaining that she had at last decided their affair must terminate. It was hurting too many people: her own children; his children; Sybil; and even the two of them.

It was a cooling off period for Burton, too. He agreed with her assessment of the relationship, and took Sybil and his children to *their* Swiss hideaway near Geneva in the Bernese Alps.

But the calm and the loneliness got to Elizabeth. "I was dying inside and trying to hide it from the children," she recalled. They were quite aware of what was troubling their mother. "I know it's going to be all right, Mama," Michael wrote her in a note. Christopher once said, "I prayed to God last night that you and Richard would be married." Elizabeth burst into tears.

Her mother and father were visiting when

Burton telephoned and invited her to lunch with him. He told her he was worried about how she was. They met at the Château de Chillon on Lake Geneva.

Burton, sun-tanned and rugged-looking, drove up and didn't see Elizabeth in the car with her parents. She saw him.

"Oh, doesn't he look wonderful?" she cried out to her mother. "I don't know what to do, I'm scared."

"Have a lovely day, baby," Sara said, and her father kissed her. Then he pushed her out of the car and she shook hands with Burton as her parents drove away.

"Well, you look marvelous!" they both chanted in unison, like a rehearsed scene. Then they laughed.

The meal was a combination of surges of conversation, and long pauses. "It was like my first date when I was about sixteen," Elizabeth recalled. But at last they began to relax and enjoy the meal. When it was over, Burton drove her home. As they parted, they didn't even kiss one another.

But it was now obvious to both of them that *Le Scandale* was not *fini*. They continued to meet, mostly for lunch. During those meetings Elizabeth's decision altered somewhat.

"I told Richard I wouldn't marry him. I didn't want him to leave his family, but I would be available if he wanted me. If and whenever he did want me, I'd be there on the other end of the phone."

It was, she said later, the biggest decision she had ever had to make. She had thought about it and decided against "playing any games" to get

Burton. In spite of the fact that she thought by making herself available she was *lowering* herself in Burton's eyes, she told him that she would be there at Gstaad if ever he wanted to call on her.

Burton later said it had not lowered her in his eyes.

During this interlude, Fox called her to make some short scenes for *Cleopatra* with Burton in Paris. By that time Burton had been assigned to do a picture for M.G.M. titled *The V.I.P.s*. During their time together in Paris, Elizabeth suggested she get a job in the picture, too. Anatole de Grunwald, producer of the picture, jumped at the chance. And, ironically enough, it was Elizabeth's old company making the picture! "They offered me $1,000,000 and 10 percent of the gross," Elizabeth said. "I figured this was a good revenge. Even I wouldn't have the audacity to ask for more." She got the million up front. She and Burton were cast as an estranged couple reunited temporarily at an airport.

The picture, in the *Grand Hotel* formula of parallel lives confined in a specific locale, takes place in the V.I.P. lounge of London Airport at Heathrow. It was at one point titled *International Hotel*. During the filming, Burton moved into a suite at the Dorchester; Elizabeth had already taken one at the same hotel. Burton's wife and children were in their London apartment; he commuted between the two sites.

Now began what eventually became called the "Dorchester Period." It was an interim calm between two storm centers, a limbo that Elizabeth described as "brimstone and fiery water." The limbo involved much activity on a professional level. Both principals were deeply involved in shooting *The V.I.P.s*. During the summer Elizabeth made a television documentary called *Elizabeth Taylor in London*.

She got $250,000 for the job, a new high for a television property at that time. The script, written by Lou Solomon and old pro S. J. Perelman, called for poetry by John Keats, Elizabeth Barrett Browning, Shakespeare, Wordsworth, and the sonorous prose of Winston Churchill. Scenes were shot in The Salisbury Pub (an actors' hangout), the original Globe Theatre, and Buckingham Palace. Produced by two Mutual Broadcasting System executives, the show was sold to CBS-TV for a reputed $1,000,000, and shown in October, 1963.

Time magazine hinted that she did it to "recoup some lost dignity." *Life* then ran a long joint interview, Richard Burton *and* Elizabeth Taylor, disguising it as a rehash of *Cleopatra*, but actually telling the world that the two lovers were together again in bed, still unmarried.

"Elizabeth and I wouldn't have been ready for all this ten years ago," Burton confessed to Jack Hamilton, referring obviously to *Le Scandale Redux*. "We met then, and carefully avoided each other. Now, we find we share the same sense of comedy and the ridiculous. That's why we love each other."

"Can you explain that we're just close friends?" Elizabeth was quoted as saying. "Nothing has been settled as of now."

Sybil had moved to New York with the children on April 2, and an American lawyer named Aaron

Frosch announced that the Burtons had become legally separated. No mention was made of divorce, although all financial arrangements were completed. Burton now proposed marriage for the first time to Elizabeth.

"Of course," she said, "I wanted to be his wife more than anything else in the world."

Burton was hired to play the lead role in Jean Anouilh's *Becket*, with Peter O'Toole as King Henry II, and John Gielgud as the King of France. In Shepperton, where the studios were located, there was a pub called The King's Head, a favorite of O'Toole's and Burton's. Burton frequently took Elizabeth there for lunch.

One afternoon a local character asked Elizabeth for her autograph.

"I will be delighted," Elizabeth told him. She reached for a menu but he shook his head. "No, no, no. I don't want you to write it on paper. I want you to sign my balls."

Wondering what kind of put-on this was, Elizabeth responded warily: "That's going to be a bit difficult, isn't it?"

"No, no," said the local character. "I've left a bit of space between Bobby Moore and John Lennon."

By this time Elizabeth was annoyed. She called over the proprietor, Archie, and wondered what was going on.

"Sign with a ballpoint," Archie said. "It's the easiest thing for signing his balls." He turned to the man. "By the way, you forgot to take them in with you."

And he went over to the bar and handed him a

couple of soccer balls.

Next on the schedule was *The Night of the Iguana,* a Tennessee Williams screen drama, for which Burton had been hired by John Huston. Screening was done in a remote village in Mexico called Puerto Vallarta.

Michael Wilding came briefly back into Elizabeth's life. Suffering from a lack of good motion picture roles, he had tried amateur painting, and was now embarking on a new and precarious career as a Hollywood agent. One of his first clients was his old friend Richard Burton.

It was Wilding who found a four-story villa high on a cliff overlooking the bay and arranged to rent it to the two of them. Burton later bought the place and maintained it as a hideaway. Meanwhile, in Puerto Vallarta, news came that Sybil Burton had been given a Mexican divorce.

He was now free to marry Elizabeth—with one small complication. Elizabeth was still married to Eddie Fisher. Fisher was reported in the press to jump in the air on hearing the news of Sybil's divorce, shouting "Marvelous! Bravo!" and breaking into a short rendition of "Guadalajara," He said that he would help his wife in any way to get a divorce.

But behind the scenes, Aaron Frosch in New York and Milton Rudin in Hollywood, now representing Elizabeth in the divorce proceedings, were finding it hard to get things moving. Fisher was holding out for a payoff of $1,000,000, they told her. She leaked it to the press.

Fisher responded, also by the press. "I wouldn't stand in the way of this earth-shattering, world-shaking romance for anything in the world," he said. "I tried for months to get Elizabeth on the phone to say let's get it over with. She wouldn't talk to me. Now all of a sudden I'm supposed to be standing in the way of the marriage of this lovely young couple who have been going together for so long."

As for the $1,000,000 he was supposed to be asking for, it was untrue. In fact, he had no idea *what* she wanted. "I'm not objecting to giving up anything. The one thing I'd like to give up is my marriage certificate. I'm willing for her to be happy with Richard the Lionhearted as soon as possible."

Then he turned philosophical. "Legal matters take time, and the great lovers will just have to bear up a few more days or maybe weeks. They stamp their feet, and if they don't get what they want, the world must stop. They're acting like a couple of kids in a playpen. They've been in their playpen long enough. They can wait a few days."

On January 14, 1964, Elizabeth filed a petition of abandonment, and the judge gave Fisher twenty-one days to reply. There was no response from the Coca-Cola kid. On March 5, Elizabeth received her divorce decree.

Burton's next assignment was to play Hamlet on the road in Toronto. The show, staged by John Gielgud, was scheduled eventually to reach New York. During the rehearsals, on March 15, 1964, he and Elizabeth flew to Montreal where the Reverend Leonard Mason, pastor of the local Unitarian Church of the Messiah in Toronto, married Elizabeth Rosemond Taylor Hilton Wilding Todd Fisher to Richard Walter Jenkins Burton in the Ritz-Carlton Hotel.

It was a very quiet, low-profile, and simple wedding, quite unlike some of Elizabeth's earlier ones.
"It was a strange anticlimax to the most publicized
love affair of the decade," wrote John Cotrell and
Fergus Cashin in their biography *Richard Burton*.
It was all over in fifteen minutes—with not a
paparazzo in attendance.

But the news made headlines everywhere, and by
the time the *Hamlet* entourage had moved to
Logan Airport in Boston, five hundred fans broke
through the police barriers and surrounded the
plane, peering in windows, screaming and waving,
making faces, and creating a mass disturbance. At
the Sheraton Plaza a thousand people were
crammed into the lobby; from the battle across the
lobby Burton received bleeding scratches on the
face.

"See if she has her wig on!" someone shrieked,
and a companion grabbed at Elizabeth's hair.
Another voice joined in: "Get some for a sou-
venir!" She even lost some of her hair to these
screaming freaks. One girl in the crowd suffered a
broken leg.

Burton grabbed Elizabeth and used his rugby
shoulders to push their way to the elevator, into
which they fell exhausted.

New York was no different. Truman Capote described one scene that greeted the Burtons as they
drove up to the theater:

"The car couldn't move because of the thousands, really thousands, of people carousing the
streets, cheering and shouting and insisting on a
glimpse of the most celebrated lovers since Mrs.
Simpson deigned to accept the King. Damp, ghost-

ly faces were flattened against the car's windows; hefty girls, in exalted conditions of libidinous excitement, pounded the roof of the car; hundreds of ordinary folk, exiting from other theaters, found themselves engorged among the laughing, weeping Burton-Taylor freaks."

The play was a big hit. Elizabeth drove down each night to pick him up after the show through the mobs of fans. One night Elizabeth was suffering a touch of flu and remained in the Regency suite. When Burton arrived home he found her watching a television movie starring Peter Sellers which she had never seen.

Burton glowered. "I was booed tonight."

"Really?" she said, glued to the set.

"Oh, turn that bloody thing off!" he snapped, sulking. "Don't you understand? I was totally booed! On the stage!"

"Yes, dear," said Elizabeth. "Never mind."

He didn't tell her it was a solitary boo from a male voice somewhere in the balcony—booing as hard as could be while all the audience cheered wildly.

Burton changed into his pajamas and returned to find his wife still entranced with Sellers on the cathode ray tube. Burton blew up, stalked across the room and kicked the set over with his bare foot. It smashed into the wall and a knob dropped off. He kicked again, this time striking the bare metal screw with his toe. Blood poured from the wound. The air turned blue with four-letter words.

Elizabeth was already holding a bandage and iodine, but unfortunately by this time she had collapsed into almost hysterical laughter that drove

Burton bananas. Next night he limped through his performance, grumbling, "Some critics have said I play Hamlet like Richard the Third, so what the hell?"

From the beginning the Burton marriage became noted not only for its moments of deep and abiding love, but for its unbelievably vitriolic fights. The Battling Burtons were so famous during the *Hamlet* period that Elizabeth related a story about a couple who had hired a room a month in advance just below the Burton suite.

"They stood up on several chairs and put empty glasses against the ceiling and listened to what was going on," she said. "I think the glasses cracked."

About their fights, Elizabeth said: "I think fighting is very healthy. It clears the air. I think there's nothing worse than one partner sulking, especially if the other person wants to get the problem out into the open and cleared away. I have quite a temper myself, so I've been told.

"Terrible fights we have. Sometimes they're in public and we hear whispers of 'That marriage won't last long.' But we know better. Even if we're in the middle of a flamer, suddenly I'll catch his eye and we give a knowing wink because we both know that once we are cuddled up in bed it will be forgotten."

Elizabeth loved to use four-letter words. "They're so terribly descriptive, they just give me a good feeling," she confessed. Burton pointed out to her that they showed a certain weakness of vocabulary. Finally he got her to promise not to use them.

"You know," she told an acquaintance, "he *has*

finally succeeded in making me stop using four-letter words."

"She's quite right," Burton chimed in. "I've cured her of that terrible habit."

"You bet your ass," agreed Elizabeth.

"A three-letter word," Burton noted hastily.

They never stopped taking pokes at one another in public. They told one reporter that they preferred pub-crawling to theatergoing for "soaking up" culture. "The truth is," Elizabeth added, "Richard has enormous taste and discretion. He can't *stand* to watch any other actor but himself."

She learned also to use her fists. During a stay in Wales, she was with Burton enjoying a drink in a pub, dressed in ski pants and blouse. One old miner looked her over closely, and said in Welsh:

"It's a funny thing, but if I had a new bloody engine, I wouldn't mind having a wrestle with her myself."

Delighted, Burton translated and Elizabeth laughed heartily—until another miner grabbed the shapely seat of her pants. Without thinking, she swung around and gave him a smart clip on the jaw with her fist.

"Oh!" crowed the miner, "look at her, Rich! Dom [damn], she's a high-spirited one!"

After *The V.I.P.*s the Burtons played together in *The Sandpiper,* a lightweight picture with the original story by producer Martin Ransohoff, and screenplay by Dalton Trumbo and Michael Wilson. In it she played a liberated woman opposite Burton's married Episcopalian minister, asserting herself against conformity by having an affair with him. Made in Big Sur on the California coast, the picture was very successful at the box office.

Judith Crist, then working on the *New York Herald Tribune,* noted that "the moral seems to be that there's nothing like a round of adultery to make a clergyman develop a social conscience." She also said, "Miss Taylor and Mr. Burton were paid $1,750,000 for performing in *The Sandpiper.* If I were you, I wouldn't settle for less for watching them."

"Miss Taylor is the best she has been in some years, while Burton is somewhat colorless," said William Peper, *New York World Telegram & Sun.* Not all the reports were that happy. John Simon, in the *New Leader:* "It is possible to get one's kicks merely out of watching Miss Taylor, who has grown so ample that it has become necessary to dress her almost exclusively in a variety of ambulatory tents. On the few occasions when she dares reveal her bosom (or part thereof), one breast (or part thereof) proves sufficient to traverse an entire wide screen frame—diagonally."

Their next picture was their best. Edward Albee's *Who's Afraid of Virginia Woolf?* was a big hit on Broadway, starring Uta Hagen and Arthur Hill. When it came to casting the motion picture, however, the Burtons won out over the original cast simply because their appearance would guarantee a total blockbuster. *Cleopatra* and *The Sandpiper* had both been big box office hits. With the Burtons, *Virginia Woolf* would be, in the words of *Look* magazine, "the safest box-office bet since Tom Mix."

Plus that, Mike Nichols, he of the comedic genius, wanted to direct it—his first movie! "That's all I'm really doing out here," Nichols clowned for the press as he appeared with the Burtons on location at Smith College in Northampton, Massachusetts, "giving the little girl her first big chance."

"He is a perverse and brilliant genius," Burton said about Nichols. "We asked him to direct this picture, and there was the natural opposition from the diehards. I said that everyone has to direct his first film sometime."

Later, about 5:30 in the morning, Burton went out and motioned the crew to gather around. Everyone came up, standing to listen to something obviously important. Burton's rolling Shakespearean inflections boomed out over the night:

"You may wonder why I have gathered you all together at this unearthly hour," he declaimed. That was all he said. He got into his car with his wife and headed home.

In more ways than one, the movie version of *Virginia Woolf* made cinema history. With a few minor exceptions, the dialogue, complete with all the four-letter words in the stage version, remained intact in the screen scenario. It was the first time that anything like that had ever been done in Hollywood.

Jack L. Warner read the script, and decided to take a chance with it. Its artistic integrity was unquestionable, as was its artistic merit. He won out over those who wanted to Bowdlerize it. Because of what Warner did, the old-fashioned movie "code" from the days of the Great Depression was abandoned entirely.

When Ernest Lehman, who wrote the screen-play and produced the movie, decided to hire both Burtons, there was mirth among the media and happy expectations of death at Warners among the competition. Elizabeth herself was terrified that she had made a mistake to sign, but Burton talked her into it.

And so the Most Beautiful Girl in Motion Pictures suddenly transformed herself into a shrewish harpy, a harsh-toned emasculator, to play Martha in Albee's play. She put on a few extra pounds—one of her happiest chores, she said later—wore a pepper-and-salt wig, and drew lines on her face.

It was, in effect, her first genuine character role.

For it, the Burtons practiced all the time—on the set and at home as well. Four-letter words split the air continually. "What the fuck?" or "For Jesus Christ's sake!" became as common as "Pass the fucking butter" in the Burton household.

It was Nichols who helped draw it out of her. He had screened all her movies and studied her closely. "The age never concerned me," he said. "The fact is that Elizabeth does know about what you could call the center of the piece, which is the intimate and possibly painful connection between people. I think that's what she did, that's what she brought." He knew she would be right for "the brilliant, over-educated, ball-cutting woman who also has woman-ly feelings and alternates between them."

Burton was uneasy about playing against his image. He underplayed the academic sadist in plastic-rimmed glasses so perfectly that he handed his wife the picture. He was nominated for an Academy Award as well as Elizabeth Taylor; she won, he did not. But *Virginia Woolf* ran off with five Oscars. Elizabeth was a smash hit.

"It is far-and-away the best Elizabeth Taylor–Richard Burton achievement to date." So said William Weaver, *Motion Picture Herald*. "Miss Taylor, who has proven she can act in response to sensitive direction, earned every penny of her reported million plus," said *Variety*. "Her characterization is at once sensual, spiteful, cynical, pitiable, loathsome, lustful and tender. Shrews—both male and female—always attract initial attention, but the projection of three-dimensional reality requires talent which sustains the interest; the talent is here. Burton delivers a smash portrayal. He evokes sympathy during the public degradations to which his wife subjects him, and his outrage, as well as his deliberate vengeance, are totally believable."

"Broadway Director Mike Nichols, in his first movie job, can claim a sizable victory simply for the performance he has wrung from Elizabeth Taylor," reported *Time* magazine. "Looking fat and fortying under a smear of makeup, with her voice pitched well below the belt, Liz as Martha is loud, sexy, vulgar, pungent, and yet achieves moments of astonishing tenderness. Only during sustained eruptions does she lapse into monotony, or look like an actress play-acting animosity instead of feeling it."

Only Andrew Sarris of *The Village Voice* saw Burton as stronger. "Without Burton the film would have been an intolerably cold experience."

Perhaps the shrew and the vixen in her had always been there under the surface. Before then, that part of Elizabeth Taylor had never been revealed to the public. And the public loved her in the part, as well as it had loved her in all her other earlier parts.

With the release of *Virginia Woolf* Elizabeth Taylor was still in the Top Ten Box Office Stars, as measured by *Motion Picture Herald*'s Annual Exhibitor Poll. The first year she reached the heights she was Number 2, in 1958 (the year *Cat on a Hot Tin Roof* was released). The second year was 1960, when she was Number 4 (the year *Butterfield 8* was released). The third year was 1961, when she moved to first place—the only time she was top of the top ten. Interestingly enough, not one of her pictures was released in 1961, but she was making *Cleopatra;* and that was the year she almost died at the Dorchester. Her fourth year was 1962 when she was Number 6; she stayed there for 1963. By 1964 she was Number 11, but back up to Number 9 in 1965 (the year *The Sandpiper* was released). She was Number 3 in 1966 (*Who's Afraid of Virginia Woolf?*), Number 6 in 1967, and Number 10 in 1968.

Since 1968 she has not reappeared. From *Cleopatra* through *Boom!* (1969) she was commanding $1,000,000 per picture. *The Only Game in Town* (1970) was the end of the big money.

The whole industry was changing.

And so were the Burtons.

CHAPTER THIRTEEN
Downward and Out

Together the Burtons made 11 motion pictures: *Cleopatra* (1963), *The V.I.P.s* (1963), *The Sandpiper* (1965), *Who's Afraid of Virginia Woolf?* (1966), *The Taming of the Shrew* (1967), *The Comedians* (1967), *Doctor Faustus* (1968), *Boom!* (1968), *Hammersmith Is Out* (1972), *Under Milk Wood* (1972), and *Divorce His, Divorce Hers* (1973), the last actually a made-for-television production.

Without Richard Burton, Elizabeth Taylor appeared in another 12: *Reflections in a Golden Eye* (1967), *Secret Ceremony* (1968), *The Only Game in Town (1970)*, *X, Y and Zee* (1972), *Night Watch* 1973), *Ash Wednesday* (1973), *Identikit* (also called *The Driver's Seat*) (1974), *That's Entertainment* (1975), *The Blue Bird* (1976), *A Little Night Music* (1976), *Winter Kills* (1977), and *Victory at Entebbe* (1978), a made-for-television movie.

But after *The Only Game in Town*, Elizabeth Taylor's box office magic was gone. The watershed picture for her as well as for the Burton team was *Who's Afraid of Virginia Woolf?* For that Elizabeth

not only won her second Oscar, but critical acclaim
as a genuine actress.

The irony was that as the public began to desert
her, her acting ability continued to grow, to
mature, and to coalesce into a true dramatic talent.
Her identity now was that of movie queen plus—
part of a new Royal Family of Motion Pictures:
The Burtons.

In the early 1960s, her affair with Burton made
both of them household words, reinforcing her
earlier fame and establishing his. But more than
that, the team made good pictures at first, pictures
that assured fabulous box office returns. The
apogee of the Burtons—talentwise as well as image-
wise—occurred in the middle 1960s—between *The
V.I.P.s* and probably as far as *The Comedians,* although their love affair with the public was beginning to wear a bit thin.

In part the problem was the selection of vehicles
to star in. But more than that was working against
the team as a life-long collaboration in the Lunt-
Fontanne tradition. Times in the theater were
changing—with a vengeance.

The 1960s brought in permissivism, activism,
and the new morality, and all its attendant ills. The
golden-age Hollywood was gone. With the breakdown of the old studio system, against which Elizabeth had railed for years, a kind of chaotic bidding system grew in its place, allowing individual
actors to lay their names on the line for millions at
the bank. When the producers found that the
Burtons were no longer attracting audiences, they
dropped them.

When they were the unchallenged King and

Queen of the cinema in the *Virginia Woolf* days, the Burtons could do no wrong. It was obvious that their dual roles in *Virginia Woolf* led to an inescapable reprise: *The Taming of the Shrew*. It was directed by Franco Zeffirelli.

Not all the critical reaction was negative. "In one of her better performances," *Time* magazine said, "Taylor makes Kate seem the ideal bawd of Avon—a creature of beauty with a voice shrieking howls and imprecations. Whenever Liz strains at the Elizabethan, the camera shifts to Burton, who catches the cadences of iambic pentameter with inborn ease."

"Elizabeth Taylor, it must be said, is no match for Shakespeare's words," wrote David Wilson in *Monthly Film Bulletin*. In effect, he bore out Burton's statement at one press conference to the effect that his wife might have some trouble with the Bard's words because " 'how durst thou' is not common talk in California."

Hollis Alpert, of the *Saturday Review*, thought that Elizabeth Taylor accepted the challenge of doing Shakespeare and succeeded at it. "In her final moments, when she is at last the tamed wife—adjusted to her situation, so to speak—she is magnificent. I don't know exactly why I felt proud of her, but I did."

But Judith Crist, at the time working for the *New York World Journal Tribune*, predictably didn't like it. "Miss Taylor, for her part, seems to be trying to make up with characterization (let alone squeals) for her discomfort with the language."

Variety thought her "a buxom delight when tamed," and Bosley Crowther warned *New York*

Times readers that "if any crusty customer doesn't like it—well, a pox on him!"

Next came a motion picture Richard Burton swore he'd someday make: Christopher Marlowe's *Doctor Faustus*. The play, even for ardent theater-goers, is a flawed one, meant more for close reading than acting. The middle has no action or story; it "just lays there" in the ungrammatical complaint of many a frustrated university dramatics director. As a movie?

The reaction to Elizabeth's role in it as Helen of Troy was predictable:

After a rap at the Burtons collectively for producing the movie—"Lots of grads bring their wives back to the old school and ham it up for home movies—but this is ridiculous. Richard Burton is charging admission."—*Time* magazine went to work on her: "Elizabeth Taylor . . . has a series of walk-ons mostly meant to exemplify lust. Her makeup varies from Greek statuesque to a head-to-toe spray job of aluminum paint. When she welcomes Burton to an eternity of damnation, her eyeballs and teeth are dripping pink in what seems to be a hellish combination of conjunctivitis and trench mouth."

Others were similar. *Variety* called it "one of the most desperately non-commercial enterprises in motion picture history." Judith Crist, now on the NBC-TV *Today* show, described it as "very high camp."

Fresh from that debacle, Elizabeth went to work on her own in an adaptation of Carson McCullers' novel *Reflections in a Golden Eye*. In it, she was to be reunited with Montgomery Clift. But two months before production began, Clift died. Burton was approached for the part, but it was that of a repressed homosexual Army major; not quite his cup of tea. Marlon Brando played the role. The picture was shot in Rome at the De Laurentiis studios, which gave the overall feeling of a rather esoteric Georgia army post.

Judith Crist: "Miss Taylor is very good as the trollopy young woman." *Time* magazine praised Julie Harris, also in the cast. *Variety* plugged Brian Keith. *Saturday Review*'s Arthur Knight: "When [Elizabeth Taylor] shrieks 'You son of a bitch!' at Brando in this one, she might still be playing *National Velvet.*" Pauline Kael in the *New Yorker* wrote: "Elizabeth Taylor is charming as a silly, sensual Southern 'lady.'" Bosley Crowther of the *New York Times* thought her "erratic," and "too often letting her bitchy housewife be merely postured and shrill."

The money kept rolling in, but the critics and the public apparently were becoming tired of these continual reprises of *Virginia Woolf*.

Next came another husband-and-wife team in *The Comedians,* an adaptation of the Graham Greene novel about "Papa Doc" Duvalier of Haiti. Largely disjointed and offering such wildly imaginative diversions as Alec Guinness in blackface drag and Elizabeth with a German accent, the picture was another non-success.

Arthur Knight in the *Saturday Review* speculated that Elizabeth Taylor was testing her loyal fans not only with *The Comedians,* but with *Reflections in Golden Eye* as well. All Bosley Crowther could say in the *New York Times* about

her was that she "appears more ferocious than usual, especially in the kissing scenes."

Feeling that three strikes didn't always indicate
an out, Tennessee Williams revived a two-time
loser, *The Milk Train Doesn't Stop Here Anymore,*
this time for cinematic adaptation. From the beginning, this story had always had title trouble. As a
short story, it was called "Man Bring This Up the
Road." In order to compress it for marquee effec-
tiveness, someone came up with the all-time nothing title *Boom!* As such, this hodgepodge contains
not only both Burtons in the cast, but Noel Coward as well, along with Michael Dunn—and Howard Taylor, Elizabeth's brother, in his first and last
appearance before cameras.

Foster Hirsch in *Cinema* hit the nail on the head.
"The film went haywire in casting a voluptuous
Elizabeth Taylor as the dying Sissy Goforth and
sagging Richard Burton as the strapping
ministrant."

Judith Crist, now with *New York Magazine,*
slaughtered everyone in it, and zeroed in on its
overall "camp atmosphere." *Variety* was cool:
"Elizabeth Taylor's delineation is off the mark: instead of an earthy dame, hypochrondriac and
hyper-emotional, who survived six wealthy husbands, she plays it like she had just lost the first."

After that unfortunate appearance came *Secret
Ceremony,* from an obscure short story involving
an aging prostitute, a psychotic young girl, and a
bearded weirdo. Sick was the name of the game.
Mia Farrow and Robert Mitchum sank in this one
with Elizabeth.

Film Daily called it "irritating" and "unsavory,"

but with a "strong impact." "What's it all about really?" asked *Film Quarterly*, with no apparent answer. The *New Yorker* found it "truly terrible."

Then came an adaptation of Frank D. Gilroy's play, *The Only Game in Town*. Warren Beatty played opposite Elizabeth in the story of a chorus girl and a piano player stranded in Las Vegas. George Stevens was attempting a comeback after he had fallen on his face with *The Greatest Story Ever Told*.

Variety liked Elizabeth, saying she had delivered "one of her best characterizations." *Cue* had her as "colorfully convincing as a lonely hoofer." "Miss Taylor, looking prettier than she has in her recent films, achieves a very affecting vulnerability," said the *Independent Film Journal*. Pauline Kael in the *New Yorker* liked Elizabeth Taylor, but thought the picture a "sluggish star vehicle of the old, bad days."

Only Game was to be Elizabeth's last for some time. Her health was beginning to suffer. She was in London's Fitzroy Suffield nursing home during the summer. Later her operation was described as the removal of her uterus. Meanwhile, Burton's star was not continuing to rise either. The day after Elizabeth's operation, director Tony Richardson fired him from the film *Laughter in the Dark*. Amid Burton's indignation over the incident, his beloved brother Ivor fell in a weird accident in Switzerland and was completely paralyzed. The Burtons simply couldn't face all their reversals and moved to their villa in Puerto Vallarta for a long rest.

They deserved it. They had enough money to last for the remainder of their lives. The Burton fortune was enormous. By this time Elizabeth's pile was estimated at more than $20 million by some and $75 million by others. Richard Burton's fortune was about $10 million, but some thought it closer to $50 million. And the seven pictures beginning with *Cleopatra* and going through *Reflections in the Golden Eye* grossed a total of $200 million!

At their peak, the Burtons made about $3,000,000 a year. But most of it vanished immediately in high overhead. A lot of it went into Elizabeth's jewel boxes. Her collection had started with Mike Todd, who came up with that 27-carat diamond. But Burton bought her a bunch more.

In 1969 what came to be known as the "Cartier-Burton" diamond was put up for auction in New York. As big as a pigeon's egg, it weighed 69.42 carats. Burton dropped out of the bidding at $1,000,000, but Cartier's went to $1,050,000 and bought it. Then Burton purchased it from the London firm at a markup. It became Elizabeth's Number One Rock.

Cartier's exhibited it to the public—"peasants," as the *New York Times* steamed, came simply to "gawk" at it. It fumed editorially: "In this Age of Vulgarity marked by such minor matters as war and poverty, it gets harder every day to scale the heights of true vulgarity. But given some loose millions, it can be done—and worse, be admired."

Number Two Rock came to her through Burton also. This was the Krupp, 33 carats in size and worth about $305,000, purchased in 1968. It was the result of a bet, the story went, and Burton called it Elizabeth's "ping-pong perfect gem" because she had won it from him by taking ten points off him at table tennis "when he was pissed."

Vera Krupp owned the ping-pong gem before the Burtons; her husband was the German munitions magnate. "I think it's charming and fitting that a little Jewish girl like me ended up with Baron Krupp's rock." Elizabeth purred.

Number Three Rock was a heart-shaped pendant that once belonged to Shah Jehan, the builder of the Taj Mahal. Worth about $100,000, it was inscribed "Eternal love till death."

Also in the running was the La Peregrina pearl, once owned by King Philip II of Spain. When he married Bloody Mary Tudor—Elizabeth I's sister —in 1554, Philip gave it to her for a wedding gift. Her jewelry box also included a 40-carat sapphire brooch, once owned by the British royal family, valued at about $69,000 (1969 prices). There was also a rare pink 25-carat diamond in a 16½ carat setting.

Jewelry only made up part of the Burton fortune. A great deal of it was in real estate. When they lived together, most of their time was spent at the Chalet Ariel in Gstaad, Switzerland—the one Elizabeth purchased during the filming of *Cleopatra*. But they also owned a big banana plantation on Tenerife in the Canary Islands. In Ireland, they owned ten acres of land in County Wicklow, where horses were bred.

The villa in Puerto Vallarta located for them by Husband Number Two, Michael Wilding, was called the Casa Kimberley. It was a favorite retreat —a white stucco Spanish-style hacienda right in the back of the village with a fabulous view of Banderas Bay. Casa Kimberley started out as one house, where they lived during the filming of *Night of the Iguana.* Later they bought another, smaller house, called their playhouse, across the street, and connected them with a bridge over the cobblestones.

The house had six guest bedrooms and a big living-dining room and terrace. The place was furnished with Columbian relics, given to the Burtons by the Mexican government.

Much of their living was done not on land, but at sea and in the air. In 1975, Burton gave his wife a hand-built Panther car, costing $25,000; she gave him a $50,000 helicopter. They both purchased their 110-foot yacht—an $850,000 ocean-going vessel that cost them $150,000 a year to tie up at a dock! It was named after Burton's daughter Kate, and Elizabeth's daughters Liza and Maria—called the *Kalizma.*

Seven bedrooms, three baths, and furnished with Louis XIV chairs, Chippendale mirrors and Empire sofas and priceless antiques, the yacht slept fourteen. A huge hand-carved mahogany bed dominated the master bedroom.

"Luv, no bunks for us," Burton told her when they began buying the furnishings.

But all the money didn't go to make life more ostentatious and comfortable for themselves and their children. The Burtons by some estimates contributed more than $1,000,000 a year to charities, not all of it tax exempt.

For example, one year Burton gave a quarter of a million dollars toward the Oxford Samuel Beckett Theater. The two Burtons then contributed to the building of a small rehearsal theater of the Oxford dramatic society. With a donation of about

$2,000 they saved *Isis*, the Oxford magazine.

In 1964, Burton announced he would set up a Richard Burton Hemophilia Fund for research. The Burtons gave from $5,000 to $10,000 apiece and made available the receipts from the charity benefit premiers of *Virginia Woolf* in Los Angeles and New York.

Way back in 1959, Elizabeth purchased $100,000 in Israeli bonds, with $70,000 in addition donated to build a theater in Tel Aviv. In 1961 she raised $7,000,000 in pledges by appearing at a fund-raiser at the Mt. Sinai-Cedars of Lebanon Medical Center. In 1966, she established a heart disease research foundation in memory of Montgomery Clift, endowing it with $1,000,000.

As the 1960s dissolved into the 1970s, the Burton marriage showed definite signs of wear. The press still called them the "The Burtons," but things were beginning to unravel behind the scenes. The reversals both had suffered in their careers and in their personal lives were putting too much pressure on a liaison that was its most effective under completely normal conditions—conditions far from the prying eye of the public.

Viewed impartially, the disintegration of the Burton-Taylor ensemble was a three-tiered matter, with three causes overlapping and blurring into one another. There was Burton's excessive drinking, there was his macho sexuality that demanded fulfillment, and there was the professional competition between the two overachieving superstars.

Burton's prodigal consumption of alcohol was legend. Filming *The Spy Who Came in from the Cold,* he was required to knock back a whiskey. "It was the last shot of the day and so I decided to use the real hard stuff." Burton grinned. "We did forty-seven takes. Imagine it—forty-seven whiskies!"

But that was a minor bout compared to an earlier drinking contest in which he was challenged by a fifteen-strong rugby team of Welsh coalminers. "I got through nineteen boilermakers —whiskey chased by a pint of beer—but next day I was in no state to remember who won."

In Mexico Burton went into local legend with a drink called the "Richard Burton Cocktail." The recipe began: "First take twenty-one tequilas . . ." The legend started on the day Burtan drank twenty-one straight tequilas and then dived fully clothed into the sea to search for a shark one of his companions claimed to have sighted.

Once asked why he drank so much, Burton replied: "To burn up the flatness—the stale, empty, dull deadness that one feels when one goes off-stage." Then, when fame had enveloped him and all but smothered him, he had a different answer. "To cure you from the agony, the idiocy of this strange world we all live in. I drink because there is no other possible way to escape the attention of the world."

Frankly, the truth of the matter was Burton drank because he enjoyed it. Elizabeth knew this. And she learned when he had had enough. She would put on what one reporter called "her hospital matron's voice," and tell him: "Richard, it's time you had a little nap."

Like his drinking, his womanizing was also legendary. Frederic March once shook his head in awe. "He has a terrific way with women. I don't think he has missed more than half a dozen."

Elizabeth knew it when she married him. But she drew the line and he promised not to cross it. "I was very bad," he confessed after ten years of marriage. "But I started a clean sheet roughly ten years ago. Since then I have never touched, never looked, never smiled at, never done anything with another woman."

Elizabeth snorted. "You're so full of rubbish. You can't help but flirt with other women. Just flirting, mind you. Anything beyond that, buster, and you'd be singing soprano by now."

Although she frequently called him "Charlie Charm," she learned to put up with most of his frequent wanderings, fobbing them off in public with a throwaway line: "Since I first met Richard he has never given me a single jealous moment."

Or another favorite: "I must say, Richard, that you have at least shown great taste i the women you marry."

As for the natural competition between two high-powered theatrical individuals, the badinage and banter became part of the Burton legend.

In the spring of 1973, the first outward manifestation of a possible break too place. The Burtons were apart for seventeen days. The, shortly after that, there was a big breakup in June. Elizabeth flew to California to visit her mother. Later they met one another in New York at the home of Aaron Frosch, the attorney who had arranged Elizabeth's divorce from Fisher. But the meeting ended in bitter wrangling and Elizabeth moved to the Regency Hotel. On July 3, she issued a statement to the press.

"I am convinced it would be a good and constructive idea if Richard and I are separated for a while. I hope with all my heart that the separation will ultimately bring us back where we should be and that is together. Pray for us."

Later on she admitted, "We were simply living too much out of each other's pockets. I love Richard Burton with every fiber of my soul. But we can't be together. We're too mutually self-destructive."

Then she flew to California where she stayed with Edith Head, a friend and confidante. Burton was playing in a film with Sophia Loren in Rome. Ponti, Sophia's husband, invited Burton to their seventeenth-century villa and there he confided in her. She tried to point out that his trouble with Elizabeth might be a simple lover's quarrel.

Elizabeth saw a lot of Roddy McDowall, her old friend, Dr. Rex Kennamer, and Peter Lawford, with whom she had worked as a teen-ager. It was Lawford who introduced her to a used-car magnate named Henry Wynberg. They met on July 6, 1973. Wynberg was an up-from-nowhere success much like Mike Todd.

A half-Jewish Dutchman, Wynberg—then calling himself Herman Wynberg—was born in Amsterdam where he worked as a bellhop until he shipped out for New York in the 1950s. He soon left the big city for the West Coast, where he worked at various jobs until he found his career as a used-car salesman. A moderately good-looking man, not very tall, and slightly chubby-cheeked, Wynberg had a great deal of appeal to women.

He peddled his charm and charisma in the posh circles of Beverly Hills, and found he could make a great deal of money selling tired iron to the rich. He used this innate charm on Elizabeth, and his attentions to her tended to relax her and improve her outlook.

Finally Burton was on the phone, demanding that Elizabeth come to Rome to see him. She hopped a private jet and got to Rome on July 23. The *paparazzi* were all over the place, snapping pictures of Elizabeth and Burton as they embraced. They drove to the Ponti villa, where the work of reconciliation commenced.

Burton was filming Ponti's *The Journey,* and Elizabeth was scheduled to do *The Driver's Seat,* an adaptation of a Muriel Spark novel, for Roberto Rossellini. Each would visit the other's set and watch the performances. All very cozy. On the surface.

She told a writer in Rome how difficult it was to love so deeply. "Just by living you inevitably hurt others. We did that in a big way when we began our life together. We couldn't help it. But what can you do—jump out of your skull?

"Sometimes I get nervous and wonder if I'm not going to pay for all of this happiness. I wonder what would happen to me if I lost Richard. Once I heard myself saying 'If you get killed or die before me, I'll never speak to you again.'"

When Burton and Sophia Loren moved to Naples for location shots on *The Journey,* Elizabeth stayed in Rome, listening to lurid stories about the two of them. Burton took Sophia aboard his yacht. Tongues wagged. Elizabeth was ailing in

November, suffering severe abdominal cramps. Wynberg appeared in Rome, flying with her to California for diagnosis. In September she was at U.C.L.A. Medical Center, having an ovary removed on which a cyst had developed.

Recuperating, she asked for Burton. He flew in.
Burton: "Hello, lumpy. How are you feeling?"
Elizabeth: "Hi, pockface."
He brought her a get-well gift—a diamond pendant. They were together once again. But they were quarreling, as usual. By mid-December they were at the Chalet Ariel in Gstaad for Christmas with the children.

Then they both split for opposite sides of the globe.

Although she was keeping her troubles to herself and presenting as calm a face as possible to the world, Elizabeth was almost completely at loose ends inside. One Sunday in early May she was scheduled to fly from Los Angeles to Philadelphia for a tennis benefit. As the airliner started its takeoff, an air speed indicator failed. The pilot turned back to the terminal.

Elizabeth left the ship, but before she got to the waiting room she became hysterical and required medication. Then she returned to her suite in the Beverly Hills Hotel. When the news hit the papers, a statement was issued:

"Miss Taylor is deathly afraid of flying, especially since her husband, Mike Todd, died in an air crash. Twice [in recent months] her planes had trouble before takeoffs. When it happened again last Sunday, she decided she didn't want to fly."

There was more worrying her than the malfunction of an air speed indicator. Quite soon the truth would come out.

The attempted reconciliation had fallen apart. An announcement appeared in the press that a divorce would be sought in Switzerland.

Two months later, on June 26, 1974, Elizabeth sat in a white dress with dark glasses over her eyes in court in Saanen while the lawyers presented the case. Judge Johanen Friedli awarded her a divorce decree on the grounds of incompatibility. In an agreement made earlier in May, she got custody of Maria Burton, their adopted daughter. There was no question about custody of her two sons by Michael Wilding and daughter by Mike Todd. She was granted rights to the Burton yacht *Kalizma*, plus her gems then thought to be worth more than $7,000,000.

"I don't want to be that much in love ever again," she said. "I don't want to give as much of myself. It hurts. I didn't reserve anything. I gave everything away . . . my soul, my being, everything . . . and it got bruised and hurt. Like a snail, I guess, I'm retreating. . . ."

Burton was holed up somewhere in New York. A doctor's certificate had been presented to the court through his attorney, proof on paper, at least, that he was too ill to travel to Berne.

Too ill? Some speculated that Burton wasn't ill at all, but simply afraid to be there. Was one of the causes of the breakup of the marriage Burton's hidden weakness? Was today's woman perhaps stronger than today's man?

Elizabeth had something to say about that theory. "A woman may dominate a man, then at times need to be dominated. . . . Really, inside herself, she wants to be dominated. She will use every wile and trick. But at the same time she is waiting for the crackdown. She wants it to come. She wants the man to take her. And she wants to lean on him —not have him lean on her.

"If he does lean on her, everything goes slightly off-key, like a bad cloud. She hopes it will pass, that the guy will come through. When it doesn't, she begins to needle him. If nothing happens she goes on needling—until he stops listening. At that moment, she becomes bitter and he goes deaf. Finally, there is no more dialogue, they have no rapport."

Max Lerner described what happened to Burton was a kind of physical and professional deterioration—whether due to alcohol, shriveling ego, or sex panic didn't matter. Lerner thought of it in terms of F. Scott Fitzgerald's hero in *Tender Is the Night.*

Burton knew he was drinking too much, but he couldn't stop it. He knew what it was doing to his acting—throwing off his timing, ruining his vocal perfection. He knew it and tried to stop, but he couldn't. He came from a family of male tipplers— grandfather, father, and now Burton himself.

He wanted her back, but couldn't get her back. Elizabeth went to Hollywood where she lived in deep seclusion. Then she began working, this time on *The Blue Bird,* a joint American-Soviet motion picture. Burton telephoned her sometimes more than twice daily—trying to effect a reconciliation.

No go. She told him how it was: "Booze, no me. No booze, me."

He tried, but it didn't work. He heard she was dating men—Wynberg, for one. In retaliation, he dated actresses, waitresses, all kinds of girls. In the fall he began going around with Princess Elizabeth of Yugoslavia, announcing on October 17 that the two of them were to be married.

When journalist Max Lerner asked Elizabeth for more details on the Princess, whom she knew, she told him she was one of her "dearest friends." Lerner wrote, "I could practically hear the hiss of the cobra humming over the telephone line."

Elizabeth admitted the Princess had a sharp tongue. Lerner wondered how long the marriage would last—*if* they married. And what would happen if Burton started wandering? "Will she give a damn?"

"She'll give a damn," Elizabeth responded.

Four months later the Princess caught Burton in Nice where he was shooting on location and going around with a former *Playboy* centerfold model, a beautiful black named Jeanie Bell. The engagement terminated, loudly and clearly, in the public prints.

Meanwhile Elizabeth continued seeing Wynberg. Lerner believed that she was using Wynberg to get back at Burton, a kind of "ultimate revenge, calculated to infuriate Burton."

Burton's liaison with Jeanie had one positive aspect to it. She got him off the bottle. By the fall he was strictly a Perrier and milk man. And so it was on August 20, 1975, that Burton would say: "Elizabeth and I may soon remarry."

It was true. Burton was scheduled to make a film in Israel. Elizabeth thought it would be "like coming home" to meet Burton in Israel.

On August 27, 1975, the story broke that the
estranged Burtons were at the Wailing Wall, Elizabeth dressed in blue jeans, Indian-style blouse,
and flowered silk head shawl, and Burton in a tan
safari suit and skull cap. There were so many fans
present that fist fights broke out in the crowd
straining to see them; Israeli police had to beat
back the screaming mob. The pair were upset and
shocked, but unhurt.

At the Wall—she on the women's side and he on
the men's side—they put their heads against the
stones and prayed. Henry Kissinger, Secretary of
State, was staying at the King David Hotel where
they had a suite, but no one seemed to pay any
attention to him. He invited them to tea, and they
came.

The still unmarried couple then flew to Africa,
arriving at Jan Smuts Airport, Johannesburg, on
September 25, where they were met by screaming
mobs of both black and white fans. They fought
their way through the milling crowd to a waiting
yellow Rolls-Royce and later attended a charity celebrity tennis tournament featuring ex-Beatle
drummer Ringo Starr and Elizabeth's old friend
Peter Lawford.

On October 10, the two superstars were in a
primitive Botswana village, and it was there that
the two of them exchanged ivory wedding rings
and were married by Ambrose Masalila, the District Commissioner, a member of the Tswana tribe.

The press around the world celebrated with the
biggest and most gaudiest headline type. "Sturm
Has Remarried Drang and All Is Right with the
World," proclaimed the *Boston Globe.* Elizabeth

was photographed clinging to Burton.

On the seven o'clock news John Chancellor used not the biggest type but his most sententious tone to announce: "Elizabeth Taylor and Richard Burton are reconciling permanently." Pause. "As opposed to temporarily." Smile.

They flew back to the Chalet Ariel in Gstaad, to settle down "for good."

They had not been married but several weeks before Elizabeth began working on Burton to return to the stage. He had not been performing for too long a time. When he demurred, she pleaded with him to take a post of don at Oxford, or to write, or to do anything to get hold of himself.

Through his agent finally he found one play. It was called *Equus*. Anthony Perkins had been playing in it. This was in the New York run. Elizabeth kept him at it right up to his opening night. And the has-been was suddenly a brand new star.

But the remarriage was coming apart. A beautiful London model whom Burton knew was staying in New York. Burton suddenly was seen around town with her rather than with Elizabeth. She was named Susan Hunt, the former wife of James "The Shunt" Hunt, a British stock car racing ace. At the Lombardy Hotel, where the Burtons were living, the arguments began to keep the neighbors awake.

In February, Elizabeth flew out to her mother's house in Los Angeles. Aaron Frosch issued a separation statement and prepared a second agreement between them.

It was all over this time—for real.

CHAPTER FOURTEEN
The Farmer's Wife

The first week in March, 1976, was a rough one for Richard Burton. He opened in a new show on Broadway and broke up forever with Elizabeth Taylor, the love of his life.

Equus was a hit; Burton was too. He was on his way up again. That was what Elizabeth had tried to do for him; she had succeeded. But she had failed to bring them together in a new life. She left him to his blond lover, Susan Hunt.

"Susan saved my life," Burton was quoted as saying. "I met her just as I was putting my hand up for the last time."

That same week there was news from another part of the world. In Malta, Peter Darmanin, an advertising executive with whom Elizabeth Taylor had been on friendly terms during the period between her two marriages to Burton, revealed to the public that he was suffering from a gash over one eye.

"That was done by a half-million-dollar ring," he told Earl Wilson. He also said that his hand was

bruised, as well as his forehead. Wilson wondered
in print if the bruise might be from a bite of one of
Elizabeth Taylor's dogs. Whatever, Darmanin told
Wilson he did not expect to hear from her again.

Actually, Darmanin and the many others linked
to her name were not the ones she was seeing. Henry Wynberg was "the man," as he had been during
the interim between Burton and Burton. With
Elizabeth's second marriage to Burton, Wynberg
had taken on a kind of Heathcliff aspect, the cast-off lover—a somehow fitting role for a used-car tycoon.

During her last days with Burton, Elizabeth was
reported to have been on the phone with Wynberg
as much as she had been on the phone with Burton
when she was with Wynberg before. Now, fleeing
Switzerland after the final decree, Elizabeth came
back to the Beverly Hills Hotel, there to remain for
some time before venturing out again.

And then, predictably, she moved in with Wynberg in his Hollywood Hills home, a place
furnished with Greek statues in the living room,
and big tanks of tropical fish along the walls. There
was a reflecting pool in front with fountains, several patios full of bird-of-paradise flowers, and a
bedroom papered with reflective silver butterflies.

The story went that the two of them had been
there before, during Elizabeth's between-husbands
period to test out the vibrations of the house, and
had found that the dark room did not bring out the
best in them. Hence the addition of the reflective
silver butterflies.

For the outside world, Elizabeth did the things
she should be doing. She went to Palm Springs to

see her mother. Then, some weeks later, she joined Wynberg on a fishing trip to Baja California. The press duly reported that she had caught no fish; no mention was made of Wynberg's catch.

Next event was the Academy Awards in Los Angeles. Halston created a strapless dress for her. In the words of the style-conscious, Halston was doing a job on her image, molding her to a more tasteful, understated elegance.

At a reception thrown by the Publicists Guild in Hollywood, Redd Foxx gave her a valuable jade ring he was wearing. Then she flew to New York and attended openings and parties and saw Liza Minnelli open in a Westchester County play.

At a fund-raising reception during Jimmy Carter's campaign she kissed him and almost blotted him out in the media reports. Even the *New York Times* mentioned her: "Elizabeth Taylor Brightens Fete for Carter."

Andy Warhol had her out to a party at Montauk where she played baseball in tee shirt and jeans. She gave out autographs to the local residents.

In Washington, D.C., she was a guest at the home of an old friend, Illinois Senator Charles H. Percy. Meeting Carl Albert, House Speaker, she asked both him and Percy to support funds for a hospital in Botswana, Africa.

She danced with Senator Edward Brooke of Massachusetts at one party. Then she had lunch with the Senate Majority Leader, Mike Mansfield.

When Elizabeth was in Israel with Burton, between-times, she had met Henry Kissinger at the King David Hotel. She saw him again briefly, in Washington. Kissinger found her an eligible bachelor—actually a divorcé—who liked to squire her around.

The divorcé was once married to the daughter of the Shah of Iran. Ardeshir Zahedi was indeed eligible, and he was a charming fellow. But religiously he was so constituted that even though he loved Elizabeth, he could never marry a converted Jewess. The press ignored this obvious fact and considered the two of them an "item." For that honor Elizabeth competed media-wise with Jacqueline Kennedy Onassis.

The Zahedi episode gave rise to some snide fun from Elizabeth's friends. Andy Warhol used the pseudonym "Firooz Zahedi" in a printed interview.

In it there was a great deal of kidding about Elizabeth's personal life:

"People very rarely ask you about your films," Warhol said. "They're more interested in your private life."

"Private?" Elizabeth repeated. "What makes you think my life is private?"

"What does *paparazzi* mean?" Warhol asked.

"Cockroach," Elizabeth shot back. "They're totally amoral and totally fearless. They're a degenerate group."

Warhol: "If you had a chance to erase some of the films you've done, which ones would you erase?"

"I have erased them so totally from my mind that I can't even remember the names. Some of them I've never seen because I knew when I was making them they were going to be disasters."

Then Warhol pointed out that Elizabeth made

the original disaster film, *Cleopatra*.

"Thank you, dear. It wasn't a disaster for me because of my overtime. The suit against me was bigger than the suit against Richard, which infuriated him."

Warhol then asked her about Washington.

"It is the hub of the universe," she responded, "and I'm still very impressed by it and impressed by meeting the people who make the kinds of decisions that influence the entire world. . . . I admire people that *do* do things."

One of the people that Elizabeth met in Washington was head of the American Revolution Bicentennial Administration. His name was John William Warner, Jr., more properly John William Warner III, since his father had been John William Warner, Jr.

Everybody was duly impressed by the name, since Warner was a name familiar to most movie goers and Hollywood luminaries. But this John Warner was not the John (Jack) L. Warner of the Warner Brothers clan. This Jack W. Warner was a Virginian.

She met him at the British Embassy during the visit of the Queen of England on the occasion of the celebration of United States' independence. Perhaps the fact that there was a strong thread of English influence running through her life made Elizabeth more susceptible at the time she met Warner.

Elizabeth Taylor soon fell in love.

Let's look at the sheet on Warner for a moment.

Born in Washington, D.C., on February 18, 1927, five years before Elizabeth was born, he was the

son of John William Warner, Jr., an obstetrician and
gynecologist, and Martha Stuart (Budd) Warner.
His uncle was Dr. Charles Tinsley (Pops) Warner,
rector of St. Albans Church from 1912 to 1949.
The rector was a highly respected and beloved
Washingtonian; his nephew was in great awe of
him.

In his early years, Warner was sent to St. Albans,
part of the complex of Episcopal churches and
schools his uncle headed up. One of the best
private schools in the country, St. Albans was
Warner's Waterloo. He started there and dropped
out three times; eventually he graduated from public school.

"I was rebellious in those days," he said later.

World War II had started when Warner was fifteen years old. "My father told me if I made the
dean's list, I could join up," he said, "so I made the
dean's list, to his surprise, I must say."

Warner joined the U.S. Navy at seventeen, and
spent the next two years—1944 to 1946—at Great
Lakes Naval Training Station near Chicago,
Illinois.He was made a cook.

The war ended before he saw any action. Once
he was discharged, he used the G.I. Bill of Rights
to enroll at Washington and Lee University in Lex-
ington, Virginia, to study engineering. He got his
B.S. in 1949 and transferred to the University of
Virginia Law School at Charlottesville, this time to
study law.

He joined the U.S. Marines at the beginning of
the Korean Conflict, and became a captain before
his discharge. He returned to Charlottesville and
graduated in 1953. For a year he went into private

practice and was appointed in 1954 to the U.S. Department of Justice in Washington. For four years he was an assistant U.S. attorney, handling murder and gambling cases.

In 1956 Warner met Catherine Mellon, the daughter of multimillionaire Paul Mellon. Catherine was a freshman at Mount Vernon Junior College in Washington. They were married a year later. By 1960 Warner was appointed a speech writer for Richard M. Nixon by Attorney General William Rogers to help Nixon into the White House. Nixon lost.

Warner then became a partner in Hogan and Hartson, a law firm with large corporate accounts. Eight years later Warner became Director of National Citizens for Nixon and Agnew. When Nixon won, that time around, he appointed Warner Under-Secretary of the Navy. Warner was considered a kind of boy wonder, being only forty-one at the time. His staff loved him: "We'd walk barefoot on glass for him," one said. But he had detractors in the media. One was Sally Quinn of the *Washington Post*, who, because of his connections with the Mellon family, always referred to him as "Secretary Watermellon."

However, he got good marks from the Secretary of Defense, Melvin Laird. "John was a team player, loyal and hardworking. He stood with us through the difficult Vietnam period." Upon the resignation of John H. Chafee in May 1972, Warner was sworn in as Secretary of the Navy.

Warner's personal life was not making the strides his professional life was. Catherine was an introverted person, with little interest in politics.

Their paths diverged and they were divorced in
1973. There were three Warner children, Mary
Conover, Virginia Stuart, and John William IV.
Although the legal agreement called for co-equal
custody, the three children—then teen-agers—
moved in with Warner. Catherine lived next door
to Warner's Georgetown house and things were
not that much changed.

As part of the divorce settlement, Warner's
father-in-law, Paul Mellon, bequeathed him a large
farm near Middleburg, Virginia, composed of
more than 2,000 acres of good farmland, including
1,000 head of cattle and a 160-year-old farmhouse
called "Atoka." Warner was appreciative of the
gift. "I have always liked farm life," he said.

The land was adjacent to a farm where Jackie
Kennedy used to go riding when she was married
to John F. Kennedy.

In the first years after his divorce, Warner dated
Barbara Walters, ABC-TV's richest female. One
story current at the time had it that he proposed
and was turned down. He also dated Barbara
Howar, another high-pressure female notable. But
nothing happened there, either.

The story around Washington had it that
Warner wanted the post of Secretary of Defense in
1974, but that General Alexander Haig maneu-
vered Nixon into appointing Warner head of the
Bicentennial Commission to clear the way for
Haig's appointment. Whatever really happened,
Warner was appointed and sworn into the job in
April 1974. The title was changed to American
Revolution Bicentennial Administration a few
months later.

During the height of the Bicentennial, Warner met Elizabeth Taylor, newly divorced from Richard Burton again.

For a time he squired her around Washington, and even took her out to show her his farm. She fell in love with it—especially Atoka—almost immediately. "I've been a gypsy most of my life," she told him. "I'm happy to have a home."

One night during an early visit, the two were walking in the fields and a thunderstorm came up. "Instead of complaining and screaming that she wanted to go home," Warner said, "Liz wanted to sit on a hilltop and watch the lightning. I thought she was special after that."

She even spoke about seeing the cows silhouetted against the moon. Her old accident-prone inclination asserted itself one day when she was riding with him; she was thrown by a horse named Big Sam, and had to be hospitalized for internal bleeding. At another time she suffered third-degree burns from an accident on a motorbike. "I don't do things by halves," she told Warner.

He proposed to her in a very short time. In fact, it was a few weeks after the Fourth of July that he produced for her an engagement ring made up of a ruby, a diamond, and a sapphire—a red-white-and-blue combination like Old Glory. Elizabeth accepted—the ring and Warner.

"I have had the privilege of many wonderful friendships in the past three years, but this is the first where I ever gave serious thought to remarriage," Warner said. "That first weekend on the farm was the beginning. Elizabeth has a wealth of personal experience and knowledge. She's traveled everywhere and known almost all the major personalities of the world."

Warner said he was attracted to her by her "real thirst for life." Talk at the time said that Elizabeth was power-mad and wanted to get into the Washington power structure. "That's wrong," Warner said. "She really wants to use her experience and some of her modest wealth for the benefit of mankind."

"I'm looking forward to a good life here," Elizabeth said.

Just prior to the wedding, which took place on December 4, Elizabeth left Vienna, where she was just wrapping up *A Little Night Music,* and flew to Switzerland to get her family so that Wilding, Todd, and Burton children could fly to the States to meet the Warner children. The actual wedding was a quiet affair, compared to some of her prior marriage rites.

Shortly afterward, the newlyweds took off on a honeymoon that included side trips to Israel, England, and Switzerland. Warner did a great deal of reading on the long voyages. When he came back he amused the media by commenting that his honeymoon with Elizabeth Taylor was memorable to him because he "got interested in Stonewall Jackson." Elizabeth's comment was not publicized.

Barbara Walters said she thought the marriage would last. "He is a genuinely nice man, devoted to his children. They each have something to give the other. He will be very good to her. He is not a man who is with one woman and looks for another. And he doesn't drink."

Others weren't so sure. "He really isn't *in* socially in Washington," a former suitor said. "He's been to Kay Graham's for dinner and to some embassy parties, but he doesn't get close to the really smart people in this town. And his pomposity can be embarrasing. He seems so determined to have a political career."

Barbara Howar didn't think Elizabeth quite understood what Washington was. "She thinks it is the Kennedy Center and embassy parties, but that isn't the inner Washington, and I'm not sure she'll be in that. John is a nice man, and if he thinks she is intelligent and what he needs, that's important."

Elizabeth Taylor's screen career continued at a much slower pace than previously. After *The Only Game in Town,* she had made *Under Milk Wood; X, Y and Zee; Night Watch; Ash Wednesday; Driver's Seat;* part of the narration for *That's Entertainment; The Blue Bird;* and *A Little Night Music.* Although Elizabeth was continuously improving her acting technique, the vehicles in which she appeared were inferior film fodder.

Under Milk Wood was Dylan Thomas's lengthy radio play transformed to film, in which she played with Peter O'Toole and Glynis Johns. It was less than a hit. *X, Y and Zee* was another commercial failure: "Go see it for Miss Taylor, a great professional who gets better as all around her get worse," said *The Guardian. Night Watch,* a stage thriller by Lucille Fletcher, was not a triumph: "Plots like this are a dime a dozen, and neither [Laurence] Harvey nor Taylor do much to rescue it from itself," said the *New York Post. Hammersmith Is Out* garnered little enthusiasm: "There is nothing to do except watch Elizabeth Taylor as a dumb

redhead act everyone else out of the picture," said
The Spectator. Ash Wednesday was another flop,
featuring a "wasted performance by Liz Taylor,"
according to *New York* magazine. *The Driver's
Seat* died a quick death, and so did *The Blue Bird,*
in which she played four parts while working in
Leningrad for months over schedule. Reviews were
mixed.

She finished work in *A Little Night Music* in Vienna just before her marriage to Warner. Her next
assignment was a nonspeaking cameo role in *Winter Kills,* based on Richard Condon's novel about a
Kennedy-type assassination. In this one she managed to get her husband assigned to a bit part.

Elizabeth plays a Washington society hostess.
Warner plays a politician being blackmailed by
her. For working one day, Elizabeth was paid
$100,000, and was given the mink coat in which she
was costumed.

According to Page Six of the *New York Post,*
when she went to director Bill Richert and told him
she wanted to keep the $10,000 coat, he said, "You
can't have it. It's a prop."

"You don't understand," she said. "I want that
coat."

Richert again told her she couldn't have it since
the company had to stop shooting because it was
running out of money. Taylor went to Warner and
told him how to handle the problem. Whatever she
told him, it worked. She got the coat.

Once they were married, the newlyweds settled
down on the farm.

"The farm is heaven," she told everyone. "It's
just the kind of life I always wanted to lead. It re-

minds me of Kent, where I grew up in England. It's the same kind of country, with rolling hills, and even the trees are the same."

Elizabeth loved to drive around the farmland in a pickup truck or to ride one of the many horses. She loved the anonymity of country life, and disguised herself in a blond wig, a red-and-white shirt and some old pants and dark glasses to go to a nearby horse race.

Within seconds a man came up to her and said, "Hello, Liz."

Another time she drove the children to an amusement part. "I took so much trouble. I took an old, beat-up truck, wore a very good wig, sunglasses and a ten-dollar dress. When I went to pay for the second ride on the merry-go-round, the man said, 'Be my guest, Miss Taylor.' I was heartbroken."

The peace and quiet of the country was fine therapy, but politics began to rear its ugly hydra head. Warner had always been involved in politics; Elizabeth had never experienced the life. For quite some time now, Warner had lusted after the office of U.S. Senator from Virginia; the seat was to be vacated in 1978. Now, with Elizabeth Taylor as his wife, Warner knew that his image would certainly be improved over the old low-profile person he had been.

He began making appearances here and there with her to get his name before the public. Warner was typically low-key at first. So was Elizabeth. But after a while both began to warm up to it. Elizabeth discovered that there was a relationship between campaigning and acting.

In a wonderfully perceptive article in the July 1977 issue of *McCall's* magazine, writer Nick Thimmesch interviewed Elizabeth.

"Political life is different," she said, "but there are similarities to show business. In politics you're responsible to the public, you're right in the public eye. I'm closer to the people now than I was when I was in films. My profession could always provide shelter, and because of my innate shyness I utilized that shelter. A lot of people mistook it for snobbism. I'm not a snob; I'm shy. But I'm learning out of necessity to overcome my shyness.

"Politics agrees with me. I relish it. But that doesn't mean that I don't get a little fussed once in a while. When I have five minutes to change clothes in the ladies' room at the air terminal, for example, or have to put on fresh makeup in the lavatory of a Greyhound bus.

"You can't feel a sense of repose when you're doing ten different things at once. It's like patting your head and rubbing your stomach at the same time. I don't see how anybody in the world can be composed and cool when they do the things we do, do you?"

But all the people weren't meek and mild because of her celebrity. "Are you here to give us an educational experience or to use your personal magnetism on Mr. Warner's behalf?" one student at the University of Richmond asked her.

Elizabeth, knowing the value of a dramatic pause, counted to ten. Then she responded, "Thank you for the magnetism bit. I'm here to share my experiences in hopes it will help someone." Long applause: she had turned that barb back onto the one who hurled it.

Another voice ased, "What is your formula for success?"

"If there were a formula, it would be bottled."

Another questioner referring to her work in *A Little Night Music:* "I didn't know you sang."

"I didn't know either." Laughter.

Another needler, with hidden reference to her $1,250,000 fee for *Only Game:* "Is Robert Redford worth two million dollars a picture?"

"Yes," she said honestly.

At one $75-a-plate fund-raiser, Elizabeth got the usual questions while Warner stood by waiting. When one reporter asked her what she thought about the fact that people were more interested in the candidate's famous wife than in the candidate, she flushed.

"John has gone out a lot on his own because of questions like that. I guess I'm more of a household word than John, but John is the candidate and I'm the candidate's wife. In show business, you're protected. In politics, you're not. You can be asked any insulting question and you have to come up with an answer."

She proved that she knew how to answer *that* question, as well as any other.

Although Warner usually was very protective of her, he would occasionally make jokes at her expense. "I have had more laughs in the past six months with Elizabeth," he told one audience, "than I had in the preceding sixteen years." He picked up a college paper and read aloud a story about how Elizabeth Taylor was a "still-trim" actress—Warner laughed out loud—with violet eyes. "Bloodshot." Elizabeth stuck out her tongue at him. There was laughter. "She is *reported* to be happy," he read on. "*Reported?*" She smiled. It was good for a warm-up.

Her acting training came in handy in sizing up reactions.

"It's not easy," she told one show business friend. "You have to be absolutely alert, on your toes and communicating the whole time. If you lapse for one second, the people can feel it. If you aren't sincere, people can sense it. You cannot allow yourself to get tired. When you shake someone's hand, look into his eyes, you have to be absolutely there."

There were the usual amusing moments, times when everything that shouldn't happen did, and times when everything that should happen didn't.

One time at an airport, Elizabeth left Warner to go to the ladies' room. He saw her waving to him from outside the door. He waved back.

They flew on to another airport, and Elizabeth again took off for the ladies' room. Warner pulled at her arm. "But, Liz, you went at the last airport."

"You damned fool, I waved at you for a dime, but you were too cheap to give it to me. This time I borrowed one from your advance man!"

Elizabeth helped Warner draw big crowds wherever he went. When Senator William L. Scott declined to run again in 1978, as had been predicted, the field was suddenly wide open. In addition to Warner, there were three other Republicans who wanted the nomination.

Front edge was given to Richard D. Obenshain. The party bigwigs didn't think much of the crowds

Warner was drawing. When it came to making their selection, they chose Obenshain, who went on to run his campaign through the beginning of the summer.

On August 3, the candidate died in an airplane crash in Richmond, Virginia. The Republican Party bigwigs met and selected Warner. Warner worked hard through the balance of the summer and into the fall. With the help of Elizabeth, he went everywhere he could go. His contender in the Democratic Party was Andrew Miller. At the time of the election they were neck and neck in the polls.

On election eve, they were still neck and neck. First count of the votes showed that Warner had beaten Miller by 4,500 votes—a mere .4 percent of the total. Miller demanded a recount. The elections committee met and informed the contenders that an election recount would cost $120,000, which the state treasury did not want to pay. Therefore, if the candidates agreed that the loser would foot the bill, the recount would be held.

Miller said that he could not afford to pay for a recount if he should lose; he called it off. It was later reported that Warner had spent $1.9 million in his campaign.

Warner was declared winner. Elizabeth Taylor was now Mrs. Senator Warner. A media report of senate wives found the majority of them to be highly indignant over being joined by Elizabeth Taylor, the *actress* and siren.

CHAPTER FIFTEEN
"Where's Stage Right?"

As the wife of the Senator from Virginia, Elizabeth Warner's life changed its focal center from the farm at Middleburg to Georgetown. Although she had thrived on the peace and quiet of the country, she was equally at home in the hustle and bustle of Washington.

She learned to field the questions of the media people so that the answers would not offend her husband's constituents—something she had never been forced to do when she was simply answering the questions asked herself as a celebrity—and she helped all she could with entertainment of political associates.

Since 1978 she had been trying to get rid of the famous Cartier-Burton diamond, which Burton had purchased for her for $1.2 million, but no one seemed to want it. It was simply that the security and insurance problems involved when she wore the diamond were too much bother. Also, it *was* a bit ostentatious for the wife of an old Virginia country gentleman like Warner.

Finally, in June, 1979, Henry L. Lambert, a long-time dealer in precious gems, purchased the 69.42 carat diamond for "nearly three million dollars." Within hours of his purchase, which was reported extensively in the press, he was approached by both foreign and domestic parties who expressed interest in buying the famous gemstone.

On a more personal level, Elizabeth decided that shapeup time had finally come. For years she had put on weight and lost it almost at will. But lately, she had been putting more on than she could take off. At a charity dinner at the Waldorf-Astoria in New York, a comedian had laced into her, making wisecracks about her plumpness, and she had broken down, to storm out of the room in tears.

In July, six months after her marriage to Warner, she signed up at The Spa, Palm-Aire, in Pompano Beach, Florida. One report said she entered at 170 pounds, but actually, she weighed only 155, according to resort officials. For her 5 foot 1 inch height, that was more than 20 pounds too much. Besides, her size 8 dresses wouldn't fit any more; she was up to 12s.

The Spa was always noted for servicing stars— Hume Cronyn, Jessica Tandy, and others. Very exclusive and very expensive, The Spa usually worked about 40 patrons through at a time. Elizabeth Warner was in good health except for her weight, according to the doctors who examined her. One described her as a "Rubenesque woman," with a smile somewhat like a "Cheshire cat." Another simply said that she had a "bloated appearance," from an "excess build-up of body flesh."

The "treatment" at The Spa consisted first of an

interview to establish the psychological reasons for excess weight, and then three weeks of physical regimen. The regimen allowed only 300 calories a day with absolutely no salt, and included exercises of several kinds, plus "special treatments."

One of the exercises was walking, starting out at a mile a day, and working up to four miles by the end of the third week. Some of The Spa exercises were working out in the pool; cooling down in a whirlpool tub; and stretching and strengthening the leg muscles.

"Specials" were twenty minutes in an herbal wrap—unbleached linen sheets steeped in a solution of blended medicated herbs; the Salt-Glo treatment, a massage with oil and salt, a hosing down, and a toning up with loofah soap scrub.

She lost twenty pounds in the three weeks she was there. When she returned to Georgetown, she was interviewed by Nancy Dickerson on television. "She's prettier than I've ever seen her in the three years since she married. She's the Liz I used to know. I'm sure her new looks will be enough incentive for her to keep on the low-calorie routine."

In the weeks that followed her visit to the fat farm, Elizabeth took up jogging, sometimes with her husband, and she could be seen frequently in the streets of Georgetown early in the morning. She lost ten pounds more in the weeks that followed.

When Ronald Reagan won the Republican nomination in 1980 and ran for president, the Warners were helping. They made the news columns more than once, and sometimes the image the Warners projected was not one of total tranquility and marital bliss. One of their frequent differences of opinion sprang from the Equal Rights Amendment. Elizabeth had always favored the amendment; Warner, with his conservative outlook, did not.

One confrontation between them in public was reminiscent of news stories that had appeared about the Battling Burtons ten years before. It took place during a political conference where over a hundred Republicans and their wives were in attendance.

Elizabeth's voice suddenly rose above the crowd during a discussion on whether or not women should be drafted. Warner had been working on a resolution favoring a draft, but excluding women.

"Don't you steady me with that old domineering hand of yours!" Elizabeth snapped when Warner tried to silence her with a wave of the hand.

"I'm sorry," Warner countered, "but you don't have a vote on this issue."

"You invited me here," she said shortly.

Warner tried to cool the argument by pointing out that he was chairman of the "Abe Lincoln Table," the one they were sitting at, and said he thought the Great Emancipator would have taken the same view on drafting women.

"Abe Lincoln?" Elizabeth repeated incredulously. "How many years do you want to go back?" History, she pointed out usually showed women taking strong roles during wartime.

"I'm proud to say when I was Secretary of the Navy I opened up more jobs to women than they had ever held before," Warner noted a bit pompously.

"Rosie-the-Riveter jobs!" Elizabeth shot back.

Another valiant Republican, Representative

Bud Shuster of Pennsylvania, jumped in to say that excluding women from registration "would discriminate in their favor."

"It all depends on the way you look at it," Elizabeth said.

Warner butted in: "Now, Liz, hold on there!" Shortly after that he left the table to discuss his resolution with someone else. When he returned he asked her what she'd been saying in his absence.

"That's for me to know and you to find out," she told him.

Largely because of press coverage of such public tiffs, and of Elizabeth's trip to the fat farm, the Warners tried to come up with some means of paring down their negative image. The obvious method was to employ a press secretary to control publicity. On August 15, it was announced that Elizabeth Taylor Warner would in the future be represented by a "public relations counsel"—the new euphemism for press agent.

Her name was Chen Sam.

Actually, Chen Sam had been working for Elizabeth ever since just before her second marriage to Richard Burton. Half Egyptian and half Italian, she was born in Cairo, and had gone to Africa where she worked for a Swiss pharmaceutical firm. When Burton contracted a case of malaria, it was Chen Sam who arrived to care for him.

She joined the Burtons' staff and traveled with them to London and Switzerland. During their stay in London, the Burtons got rid of their business manager and took her on. "It came as sort of a surprise," she said. "I couldn't even type."

When the Burtons broke up for the second time, Chen stayed with Elizabeth. By the time Elizabeth

had married Warner, Chem Sam was running a
public relations firm called Chen Sam & Associates
in New York. Among her clients were aspiring actress Maria Burton and poet Rod McKuen—and,
of course, Elizabeth Taylor.

Uncontrollable publicity is the problem of any
personal manager or press agent, and Elizabeth
had always been subject to the worst kind. The two
most common questions about her were her personality and her eye color—plus those about her
weight problems and her squabbles with her husband.

Apparently Chen Sam did some good, because
the stories began to cool off a bit, and there were
none quite so detailed about the Wrangling
Warners as there had been about the Battling
Burtons. In fact, in the 1980 elections, the Warners
helped the Republicans to win. Or, at least, they
did nothing to hurt Reagan's chances.

Elizabeth did have one narrow escape on the accident front, however. During a campaign swing
through southwest Virginia, the Warners visited
the kitchen of a restaurant in Big Stone Gap. The
chef was proud of his chicken and wanted Elizabeth to sample some. Afraid to demur because it
might hurt Warner's image, she took a piece and
began chewing.

Somehow the chicken bone—two inches long—
got lodged in her throat. She was rushed to Lone-
some Pine Hospital where it was removed without
resort to surgery. Nevertheless, it was a scary moment. She was kept under observation for a respiratory ailment she was suffering at the time, and
then released.

With the Reagans in the White House, Elizabeth began to turn away from politics toward show business again. John Springer, her agent, would still send her scenarios to read, but she was so slow getting to them that when she finished reading one, indicating that she might do the picture, Springer would have to tell her: "Elizabeth, darling, that's already been filmed now."

Finally Zev Bufman, a Broadway producer, got in touch with Springer. The Broadway stage was a brand new challenge for Elizabeth Taylor, but she thought she might try it. Besides, Warner began encouraging her to try it—it was something new.

It was also something with a little more prestige than motion pictures. Warner was still smarting over the fact that Senate and House wives had protested the inclusion of "movie star" Elizabeth Taylor among their sanctified selves.

In addition to that insult, Warner had been dropped from the Social Register back in 1977 after his marriage to Elizabeth Taylor; no reason was of course given for that—but it all seemed rather obvious.

"It was my husband's idea that I do a play," Elizabeth told her colleagues later. "I've campaigned so much in the last four years. He wanted me to do something of my own."

Bufman had two plays that he thought suitable for Elizabeth Taylor. They were revivals, old standards, not new properties. One was the sparkling Noel Coward comedy called *Hay Fever;* the other was Lillian Hellman's Deep South drama *The Little Foxes.*

Readings were held for the two plays. After the

runthroughs it seemed obvious to both Bufman
and Elizabeth that the Hellman drama had it over
the Coward play. For one thing, the part of Regina, while not exactly specifically Elizabeth Taylor, was close to the kind of role she did best.

"Regina is not just a total icicle, an avaricious
bitch, as she is usually portrayed," Elizabeth noted
after studying the script. "I've found so many
facets in her. There is also a certain vulnerability in
Regina."

Bufman noted that Elizabeth's two play readings
were the first time a play had been auditioned for a
star. The decision was soon made, and the schedule
was drawn up, with the New York opening originally scheduled for April 30, 1981, after out-of-
town tryouts in Fort Lauderdale, Florida, and
Washington, D.C. Elizabeth Taylor's salary was,
according to Bufman, "higher than normal."

Immediately the cast was assembled, including
Maureen Stapleton, Tom Aldredge, and Anthony
Zerbe filling the pivotal roles. Austin Pendleton
was hired to direct.

The signing of Elizabeth Taylor was a real coup
for Bufman, he told the press; she was the strongest
draw he had ever presented on Broadway. One reporter wondered if Elizabeth Taylor would be worried about what the critics said.

"I've been rapped enough by movie critics, and I
can take it," she responded. "If you're rapped by
theater critics, what's the difference?"

One thing that did worry her from the start was
memorizing her lines. She had always been a quick
study, but in motion picture production, the takes
were always very short. In a play, she was required

to know *all* the lines letter perfect.

"What happens if you forget your lines?" she asked the other actors. "No matter how well you know your lines, you can still go blank. That is a frightening thought to me."

No one ever really gave her an answer.

Another challenge was voice projection. On the set she always spoke in a natural voice with a microphone nearby. Onstage there was no artificial help. She began working on it. "I asked the other actors if I'll need any special coaching, but they didn't think so."

As for changing her style of acting from camera work to stage work, she was quite sanguine about it. "I feel acting is acting. You just have to make modifications. In a film, the audience is only a foot away. On stage . . ." She waved her arm.

From the beginning, she got into the spirit of the thing. She knew her lines, she did what she was told, and at the same time she could clown around when things got monotonous.

Pendleton once told her: "When you enter the dining room on this set, I want you to come in from stage right."

"Stage right?" Elizabeth asked in horror. "What's stage right?"

Anthony Zerbe looked astounded. "You can't be a star if you don't know stage right!"

Elizabeth shrugged and giggled.

And she could be petulant and very snippy too, when she felt like it. One of the cast complimented her one day on her loss of weight. "Does it matter what Maureen Stapleton weighs?" she snapped. "What does it matter what *I* weigh?"

Shortly before the tryouts in Fort Lauderdale,
the Warners rented an 82-foot yacht in Miami and
invited the entire cast to a party. Elizabeth showed
up dressed in a stunning outfit, wearing the famous
Krupp diamond. When she showed it to one of the
cast members, she cautioned: "Don't cut yourself
on the facets!"

That led her to expound on diamonds. "I think
what I love is the perfection of the diamond itself—
and that's nature. It's something so perfect that
you have to enjoy it or you're very jaded."

Somewhere else on the yacht Maureen Stapleton
was philosophizing about Elizabeth Taylor and
what she had been through in her life. "It's because
she has been a survivor of so many things, and
she's done her surviving under such public
scrutiny."

The tryouts proved encouraging. The critics
were generally positive. "She has a definite presence (enhanced by Florence Klotz's low-cut costumes) that makes her as effective on the stage as
she is on the screen," said the *Baltimore Sun*. "As
for Miss Taylor, she does as well as could be expected with what she has to offer. The trouble is
that what she has to offer is not what the role requires."

Paul Healy noted that her "accent as the Dixie
spitfire Regina comes and goes like a Southern
breeze."

By the time the Florida stand was finished, the
play was a sell-out in New York for the entire
10-week schedule, beginning now on May 7, with
preview performances a week before.

The Washington tryouts were something else

again. One observer commented that the first night in Washington brought out an audience that looked like a magazine ad for Chivas Regal—all sequins and taffeta.

The President and First Lady attended. Nancy Reagan was of course a contract player once named Nancy Davis at M.G.M., the same studio where Elizabeth Taylor worked. They renewed their acquaintance in public, both women quite different now from those days back in Culver City.

Then the play moved to New York. Before the opening there was a big pre-theater party. Elizabeth's mother, calling herself Sara Sothern Taylor now, was present, along with Elizabeth's daughter Maria Burton. Rock Hudson flew in from the Coast with Claire Trevor; both were old friends. "They're going to kill me," Elizabeth predicted to Claire, making a knifing sign with her forefinger across her throat.

"Don't be silly. You'll be a smash."

The day before opening night Elizabeth was suffering from a throat infection and high fever. Several of the early preview shows had been cancelled because of her 102 degree fever.

"I'm using all my will power to get over this," she said. "No matter how sick I am, I will go on for the opening. I won't cancel it, even if I am croaking."

Dr. Wilbur Gould, otolaryngologist to the biggest Broadway stars, pointed out that she had been sick four times with pneumonia in the past, and that she was allergic to antibiotics.

"It's so ridiculous," Elizabeth said. "I feel pretty sick, and I'm furious. We've been working so long, and we're on such a high. It's very bad luck."

She did appear, and the play was a smash. After the show she made the traditional appearance at Sardi's. When she entered in a white Halston gown with a plunging neckline, a red shawl over her shoulders, and diamonds and pearls, the entire restaurant stood up and applauded. The place was packed with celebrities: Hudson, Trevor, Sara Sothern Taylor, Bill Blass, Peter Strauss, Irving Lazar, Lee Radziwill, Joan Fontaine, Cicily Tyson, Andy Warhol. Even Halston later walked in alone, in a cloud of fragrance.

Joan Fontaine said: "Well of course I love watching Elizabeth in anything. We started together, you know, in *Jane Eyre*. Oh, years ago."

By then the reviews had begun to come in. The party picked up in spirit. They were mostly good—better than at the tryouts, actually.

The *New York Times* reviewer, Frank Rich, said the performance began "gingerly, soon gathers steam and then exploded into a black and thunderous storm that may just knock you out of your seat." He thought it "just the right vehicle" for her, played in the proper "high style."

"Miss Taylor's moneyed tone—a little grating, a little agitated, more than a little fiery—is just right for the character of Regina Giddens." And the capper: "Elizabeth Taylor . . . looks very much like someone who's on the stage to stay."

The *New Yorker* was the pleasantest surprise of all. "In New York last week, there appeared to be but a single question worth asking: What would Elizabeth Taylor make of the role of Regina Giddens in "The Little Foxes"? Happily, the answer is that she makes an excellent thing of it. . . . She seems perfectly at ease on the stage of the Martin Beck and readily holds her own in the presence of such seasoned troupers and scene stealers as Maureen Stapleton and Tom Aldredge. The fact that she is what is commonly called a superstar . . . casts no taint upon the nature of her performance, which is well thought out and skillfully modulated. . . .

"Tallulah Bankhead, who first played Regina (it was the finest role of her career), cannot have spoken the tremendous last lines of the second act any more effectively than Miss Taylor does. They are like repeated blows in the face, and the audience gasps at them, in mingled astonishment and pain. . . .

"She is a dynamo that shows not the least sign of running down."

The *Christian Science Monitor* thought her effective, too. "In her theatrical debut, one of Hollywood's legendary glamour ladies bestows her considerable presence, power and acting acumen upon one of contemporary American drama's prize villainesses. With Elizabeth Taylor starring as the vixenish Regina Giddens, 'The Little Foxes' luxuriates in a kind of timeless grandeur well suited to Lillian Hellman's 1939 play."

In the *Monitor* critique, John Beaufort went on to say that the role itself had little depth. "What Miss Taylor does is to endow the part with her particular aura. This Regina is a wickedly handsome predator. Because of Miss Taylor's presence 'The Little Foxes' is already a financial success, being virtually sold out for its initial 10-week run."

Clive Barnes in the *New York Post* wrote, "There is a magnificent presence here by Elizabeth Taylor. The sheer punch aura of stardom that is totally undeniable and unmistakable. When she walks on stage it lights up, and the audience basks in its reflection."

CBS-TV's Dennis Cunningham: "Elizabeth Taylor triumphs! She's glorious in a thoroughly first-class production. Elizabeth Taylor breezed in as a Queen of Broadway. God Bless her, I say, and long may she reign! *The Little Foxes* is a marvel and beyond that a shimmering entertainment! A shimmering event, in fact!"

And more:

Liz Smith, *Daily News* Syndication: "Elizabeth Taylor in *The Little Foxes* is marvelous. She is a great presence, a great lady and a great pro. Welcome to the theatre!"

NBC-TV's Katie Kelly: "Elizabeth Taylor making her Broadway debut looks terrific! Miss Taylor grabs the wheel, steers a straight course to the finish line and never misses a light. Hats off, Liz, you did it!"

Newsweek was almost ecstatic: "As Taylor makes her entrance, what we see is beauty—the mortal beauty of gallantry in action. The 49-year-old Taylor carries the geology of her life—the lush body of the mature sybarite and the baby face of the stardusted child. Faced with such a dramatically psysicalized fate, who wouldn't be moved? You can almost feel the ultraviolet rays from the legendary eyes."

Even *Time* whistled. "Elizabeth Taylor is something to watch," wrote T. E. Kalem. "In air and bearing, she possesses regal command. Her arrant good looks, particularly those thrust-startled eyes, fix all other eyes upon her. On glimpsing her, Poe might have written his poem 'To Helen,' apostrophizing the most beguiling beauty of the ancient world. QE2 (as someone recently nicknamed Taylor) conjures up that grace and grandeur."

Later on, Walter Kerr wrote a thoughtful piece for the *New York Times* Sunday drama section which tackled some of the problems that most of the critics didn't bother to mention. He analyzed carefully several lines which were spoken by the star to elicit laughs rather than thought.

One such misplaced laugh came, according to Kerr, in a discussion between Regina and her husband, Horace. Regina, frustrated by Horace in a business manipulation, tells him that she has always felt contempt for him.

"From the very first?" he asks tentatively.

Pause. "I think so," she replies.

Big laugh.

"It's the wrong laugh in the wrong place," Kerr wrote. "Regina . . . intends to be *productively* mean. She isn't playfully pretending to put a precise date on her first loathing for Horace as a way of idly amusing herself, or of entertaining us. She's trying, with the cutting edge of those few words, to produce an effect on Horace; to shock him, to freshly dismay him, to humble him and bring him to heel." If laughter is provoked, Kerr noted, it must be black laughter, laughter with a bitter chill embedded in it.

The laughter here "upends the situation, contradicts our actual sympathies, reverses the relationship of the two figures on stage. A laugh that stands the play's meaning on its head is obviously a laugh that needs to be tempered, reshaped. Why hasn't the actress sensed that, why does she so often settle for quick small victories while she is losing the big battle?"

Kerr's answer: "I think because . . . she is one of those performers who can make bold and striking use of their own personalities but who have no knack at all for slipping inside an imagined character's skin and staying there long enough to see and feel the world as that character might. . . .

"The lady hasn't measured her effect in terms of what good it will do the play. . . . The bits and pieces don't attach themselves to a single intelligible *person,* growing in complexity and power before our eyes."

But Kerr was almost alone in his dissent. And in spite of whatever dissents there were, the public came in droves. Yet try as she might, Elizabeth was still unable to shake the various ills that continued to dog her.

On opening night she had a fever of 102 degrees, but Dr. Wilbur Gould let her go on after dosing her with medicine. Then, a week after the show opened, on May 16, Maureen Stapleton was sitting in her dressing room, putting on her makeup, when someone stopped at the door and looked in at her.

"For a split second," she said, "I didn't know who it was. Then I saw the blue jeans and I realized it was Elizabeth Taylor." The star was so ill that she could hardly stand. "I gave her a seat where she couldn't see herself in the mirror."

She appealed to her to call the performance off, but Elizabeth refused. After a long argument, she finally got to her own dressing room where the makeup crew attended her. She did not recover, and when suddenly she turned white and fell off the chair to the floor, the decision was taken out of her hands, and the show was cancelled.

She was rushed to Lenox Hill Hospital where her condition was diagnosed as a combination of severe respiratory infection and a torn rib cartilage caused by excessive coughing from the infection.

"Everytime she coughed it was like a knife going through her," explained Pendleton. Maureen Stapleton praised her guts. "She will do it till she drops," she said. "In no other profession in the world do you work when you are sick. Try getting the plumber when the plumber is sick."

Stage manager Patrick Horrigan read a brief statement to the audience, telling them that the star's cartilages were inflamed and that she was "in pain as severe as the human body can endure."

Two days later she was back, cured after a good rest.

Again, in early June a 24-hour virus struck her, and the performance had to be cancelled. But the effort she put into it proved worthwhile. Elizabeth Taylor played out her 10-week run, and then took the show on the road.

When the Tony Awards were given in June, Elizabeth Taylor was nominated, but was up against stiff competition: Maureen Stapleton; Jane Lapotaire for her portrayal of Piaf; Glenda Jackson, Eva Le Gallienne; and others.

Although the inside word was that she didn't

have a chance against such veterans, a lot of people wanted her to win. One of them was Maureen Stapleton, who had become a good friend during their work together. "She's a big number, a natural, and I hope she wins!"

Elizabeth lost out to Jane Lapotaire. But she applauded the winner, and then said she was giving a party for all the Tony losers at Sardi's after the awards ceremony was finished. "I believe Elizabeth would have won Miss Popularity had there been a contest," Earl Wilson said.

"Thank Elizabeth for the boom she brought to Broadway!" one insider said. Her own agent, Robby Lantz, noted that Bette Davis had once defined a star as "an actor who sells tickets." Lantz went on: "Elizabeth is selling every ticket available."

More than anything else, she had proved to some of the toughest critics and professionals in the world that she was as much a Broadway star as a motion picture superstar.

CHAPTER SIXTEEN
The Supporting Cast

Except for Richard Burton, most of the people who have been close to Elizabeth Taylor have been quite simply overpowered by their nearness to her fame. Those who suffered the most were her children.

"Children are the true wealth," Elizabeth once said. She also said, "To me the most beautiful smells in the world are babies and bacon." The image of the proud young mother who was always with her children was hers during her early years. Photographs printed in the newspapers showed her clutching her baby as she got on and disembarked from airplanes.

Her offspring seemed to be substitutes for the animals with which she had originally surrounded herself as a child. Yet at no time in her life did she really take to cooking, as the statement about "babies and bacon" might imply. There was always someone else who did that for her. And there was someone there to care for the children, too.

"But still, at the same time," a magazine article
said in 1956, "she is many of the things the girl next
door should be. She is a wise and conscientious
mother, a devoted wife, a person of dignity, humor, and abundant common sense. . . . When she
relaxes, she does so completely . . . making up to
her sons for the days she must spend away from
them."

That was the image that was projected, and it
was the public image M.G.M. wanted for their valuable property. The truth was a bit different. One
dinner guest once summed up her motherhood as
follows: "They [she and Michael Wilding] had
those two *terrifying* boys."

Nevertheless, during the early years, the Wilding
boys—Michael Jr. and Christopher—presented
few problems that were visible to the media. That
was years before the 1960s and the 1970s, when
things changed.

Michael, born in 1953, grew up just as the world
entered the revolutionary 1960s. He took on all the
aspects of the permissive generation, joined the
subculture, wore his hair long, pierced his ears and
inserted gold earrings, and dressed in caftans, love
beads and medallions.

He preferred living in England to America.
When he was seventeen, he decided to marry an
English girl named Beth Clutter, who was a key-
punch operator. She was older than he. They were
married where his mother had earlier married his
father: at London's Caxton Hall Registry.

As a wedding present, he was given a $78,000
house by his mother and stepfather—at that time
Richard Burton. The couple had a son in 1971, and

seemed about to settle down in the London townhouse as a normal family.

In England as in America the countryside was sprouting communes for what came to be called "the hippie culture" through the 1960s. After a few stormy months in London, Michael and his wife opted for the "true life" and gave up the house to go live in a commune in the Cambrian Mountains.

Beth Wilding didn't think much of the commune, but there was nothing she could do but follow Michael and the baby. Michael decided that the whole scene in America—the Vietnam War, the conformity, the reactionary government—was too much for him. He renounced his United States citizenship.

Two years later he was in the newspapers again. He had split up with Beth. The divorce came through in 1974, and was duly reported. Meanwhile, he had moved to another commune, this one in Wales not far from the village his stepfather came from.

There he met another woman, this one named Johanna Lykke-Dahn. He moved in with "Jo." He was fined $120 by the police for growing marijuana on the farm where the commune was located, and made the public prints again.

He and Jo had a little girl. Several of the commune members got together to form a rock group called "Solar Ben." The versatile Michael played flute, trumpet, and guitar.

One commune resident was unimpressed by Michael Wilding, who claimed to be the son of the famous Elizabeth Taylor. But after the birth of his second child, Elizabeth visited the commune and the unbeliever was convinced.

"She sang to the infant as she held it in her arms," he said. "I'd venture to say that she actually liked being a grandmother." There was no mistaking that face, he said. "Michael does resemble her a great deal."

Burton was never too taken with his stepson Michael. He hated to see what was happening to him. It had taken Burton such a lot of energy and muscle and guts to climb up out of the filth and backwash of the Welsh coal mining area where he was born that he deeply resented anyone who would give up the good things in life to go back to the pits again.

"I made it up and the boy's trying to make it down." He shook his head. "I get so goddamned mad when I think of what it took me to climb out."

As for the second Wilding boy, Christopher, he grew up to be a handsome and charming young man who was once considered for the role of Jesus in a projected television play of the *Life of Christ*. He didn't make it because the casting director thought him too young.

During his teens, Christopher had developed into a pretty good sketch artist—hardly a surprise considering that the Burtons at one time owned dozens of classic originals by such masters as Van Gogh, Monet, Renoir, Utrillo, Pissarro, Degas and Modigliani, among others. Or that his father was a painter as well.

When Christopher visited his father—Michael Wilding—then living in Chichester with his wife Margaret Leighton, Christopher did a number of drawings of the countryside. They were left with his father in the cottage there.

In spite of his artistic bent, he was never too interested in wearing long hair and dressing up in jeans and love beads like his brother Michael. Instead, when he got the chance, he joined up with his Uncle Howard—Elizabeth's brother—in Hawaii. Howard Taylor had become a professor of oceanography during the years his sister was world-famous and/or infamous.

In Hawaii he enrolled at the University of Hawaii, where he managed to compile a fairly good record. He was almost the mirror opposite of Michael, being obviously a conformist, and perhaps a square, and enjoying it.

"He's a very level-headed, sweet guy," one of his classmates said. "He's the sort you select to be the referee, because you know you'll be sure to get a fair shake."

His mother always did approve of Christopher. "I don't know if he will ever get to be President or Prime Minister, but if he doesn't, the people will be the poorer. He's the fairest person I know."

After graduation, Christopher moved back to the mainland. By this time his interest in art had altered slightly to a focus on photography.

In July, 1979, he was married to Aileen Getty, one of the famous Texas Gettys.

The third of Elizabeth's children, Liza Todd, grew up, like Christopher, with a pronounced interest in art *and* sculpture. But there were additional attractions in Liza's makeup. She possessed two of the most desirable characteristics from her mother and father—her mother's looks and her father's personality.

This magnetism and energy tended to distract her from her quiet studies at Middlesex

Polytechnic School in London. However, she continued to turn out all kinds of creations which her mother put into her houses in Switzerland and Mexico.

"With her heritage," one Hollywood insider said, "she'll have a difficult time avoiding the movies."

Elizabeth's fourth child, Maria Burton, was actually adopted at the time Elizabeth was married to Eddie Fisher. An infant with a malformed hip, she suffered from malnutrition until she was taken over by the Fishers. A series of complicated operations were performed on her to correct the problems in her hip.

As she grew up, she became as normal physically as anyone else. She lived mostly in Geneva, Switzerland, loved skiing, and came over to America to be with her mother when Elizabeth married Warner.

Maria had aspirations toward either the stage or motion pictures. She signed up with Chen Sam, who had become her mother's public relations counsel, and began appearing with her mother whenever she could.

So much for the children. But what about the husbands?

First, let's take a look at another level of supporting characters. One of Elizabeth's best friends after Roddy McDowall was Montgomery Clift.

McDowall, incidentally, continued on his acting career, appearing even in the greatest disaster picture of all time, *Cleopatra*. He kept on in motion pictures, on the Broadway stage, and in television. He and Elizabeth continued to see one another whenever they could.

Clift went the other way. His dependence on

drugs and alcohol was increasing rather than decreasing; his troubles in filming *Suddenly Last Summer* were not the end of it. Nothing had been the same after his automobile accident.

Truman Capote ran into him during the 1966 Christmas season. They had lunch at Le Pavillon where Clift had a few martinis. Not many months later, Clift was dead.

As for the husbands:

Conrad Nicholas Hilton died on February 6, 1969. His life after his divorce from Elizabeth Taylor was not particularly exciting.

Michael Wilding never did make it back into motion pictures after his divorce from Elizabeth. Instead, he took up painting for awhile, but then decided that he couldn't quite make a living at it.

He became a Hollywood agent—probably the lowest point of his life—and then left the States for England. He eventually married the English actress, Margaret Leighton. They lived a happy if uneventful life in the English countryside that Wilding loved so well.

He died on July 20, 1979. Elizabeth and the boys went to the funeral.

Mike Todd of course died after just a little more than a year of marriage to Elizabeth.

Eddie Fisher fled the Rome scene when it became evident that his wife was more interested in Richard Burton than in him. The marriage had been going sour for some time before that, anyway, and Fisher was afraid his career was on the rocks.

He was right. The 1960s was a time when the old way of singing was going out, never to return. Fisher was essentially a crooner; he had always been influenced by Frank Sinatra's style of delivery. Now, with the English Beatles coming in, and hard rock on the horizon, it was tough to make money selling records of ballads.

Fisher took up with an actress named Connie Stevens, who had played in a television series called *Hawaiian Eye*. They had a baby, and eventually Fisher married her. But the marriage didn't take. They had another child. Fisher soon left.

He was once asked which of his three wives he would like to see perform: Debbie Reynolds, Elizabeth Taylor, or Connie Stevens. "Elizabeth Taylor was the love of my life," he said quickly. "I never considered her a performer."

In 1967, Fisher teamed up with comedian Buddy Hackett and made a few appearances that put some money in the pot. But by 1968 Fisher's "injections" had turned him into a hopeless addict; he was on a sequence of uppers in the morning and downers in the evening.

Connie Stevens divorced him, and he went from one woman to another. In 1970, there was an investigation of Dr. Max Jacobson, followed by a sensational exposé; he had been mixing vitamins and hard drugs for the celebrity trade. He was suddenly out of business.

Fisher tried to shake his drug habit "cold turkey" in Jamaica at the Kingston Hilton. He almost died. Back on the drugs, he tried another comeback. He married again in 1975, and one year later, on another comeback with Hackett, he had a loud, tasteless quarrel with him onstage in public, and that was the end. That same year a close friend of Fisher's, one of his drug buddies, was found murdered. Fisher was questioned but not held.

Gwen Davis, a journalist and novelist, visited

Elizabeth Taylor in 1976 for a piece she was doing for *McCall's*. Elizabeth was in traction at the time, suffering from a back problem. Later, in the winter she went to see Eddie Fisher singing in a restaurant in California.

"I was saddened by his appearance," she wrote. "I wondered where the boy had gone. I realized that one of the true inequities of life was that Elizabeth Taylor looked better in traction than Eddie Fisher did in a restaurant."

"Survival is my philosophy," Fisher was quoted as saying. "I don't like people, I like individuals. I like audiences."

Richard Burton married Susan Hunt shortly after his second divorce from Elizabeth became final. He had tried to get a divorce in a court in Haiti in June, shortly after Elizabeth flew to the Coast for the last time. But his papers weren't in order. After sweating it out for a few weeks, the papers eventually did come through, and the divorce was granted on July 31.

Burton flew with Susan Hunt to Arlington, Virginia, and was married to her on August 21, 1976. He had no need for a comeback; he had more money than anyone in the Jenkins family had ever dreamed of having.

The stage always called. Eventually, and ironically, he made a comeback on Broadway in *Camelot,* his favorite vehicle, just weeks before Elizabeth Taylor opened in *The Little Foxes.* But he had trouble; eventually he had to leave the show for an operation to relieve a chronic spinal condition.

He took the show on tour and was on tour when *The Little Foxes* opened.

"Some friendships dwindle away," Elizabeth Taylor once said. "Some remain as genuine, even if you haven't seen the person for five years."

She was referring to a handful of people she liked to visit on the West Coast when she went out to see her mother: Roddy McDowall, Rock Hudson, Nancy Walker, Liza Minnelli, and Sammy Davis, Jr.

Joseph L. Mankiewicz once said that "the principal role in Elizabeth's life has always been to be a wife of the man she's married to."

Mankiewicz then pointed out that Elizabeth Taylor's earlier life did not include any growing-up trials and errors, the way the lives of other people did. She played the roles someone else concocted for her; she said the lines someone else wrote for her. Her standards were set by M.G.M.'s script writers.

"If you love your lover," Mankiewicz said, "you take him by the hand and confront the world openly with him." That was a standard formula of the time. When Elizabeth did exactly the same thing in real life, "she got belted right in the puss. But when she did it on the screen, she was a great star."

He paused. "This makes for tremendous confusion."

But Elizabeth Taylor learned how to cope anyway. "She's been whatever the script calls for. The thread that goes through the whole is that of a woman who is an honest performer. Therein derives her identity. If she's a success at that, she's totally invulnerable."

Over the years Elizabeth developed a philosophy of life and a method of coping with problems that came up.

"I think I can take criticism very well," she said, "but I still don't know how to take a compliment. I suffer acute embarrassment. I don't know what to say so I usually end up by making some feeble crack which is ungracious and makes the other person feel bad. I know it, I'm aware of it. I get all tied up in a terrible knot and mumble thank you. It seems as if I'm indifferent, but it's just that I simply don't know how to accept a compliment."

Many of the compliments had to do with her beauty. But perhaps beauty was an overrated commodity.

"I don't know whether my 'beauty' has been a disadvantage or not. I have never considered myself a beauty. When I was young I suppose I was pretty, but it was a disadvantage in a way, as I was always typecast. Men react superficially to beauty. I think I can tell if the vibrations are genuine. If it's just flattery, I find it condescending.

"People who worry about their looks and their figures and all that lose what really makes a person. If you spend all your time worrying about how you look, then you are living totally within yourself. All I see when I look in the mirror is a dirty face, an unmade-up face, or a made-up face.

"It's better to forget about keeping beautiful through diets and health farms. Enjoy life—it's much more important. No matter what people look like physically, some can have an inner glow and vitality much more beautiful than a 36-22-36 figure."

As for inner discipline: "I still have no sense of time. It's like a disease. If I could conquer it I would be fairly disciplined. It isn't deliberate. It isn't a subconscious rebellion. I think it began during my younger days when I had to go both to work and to school, and I would much rather have been out riding a horse."

Throughout all the trials and tribulations, Elizabeth Taylor did eventually manage to evolve a simple philosophy of life.

"I'm a fatalist in my own personal life. I try to live and enjoy every moment as it exists. Think about tomorrow but don't worry about it. It may bring ten different things but nobody knows what they are until tomorrow.

"I'm not a worrier about things like that. I really enjoy life. I relish it. I enjoy *now*! If I had to write my own epitaph it would be: 'Here lies Elizabeth Taylor. Thank you for every moment, good and bad. I've enjoyed it all!'"

At the time of this writing, Miss Taylor and her seventh husband, Senator John Warner, have agreed to separate. Also, Miss Taylor appeared in the highly rated daytime soap opera GENERAL HOSPITAL (her personal favorite) and donated all of her earnings on the show to charity.

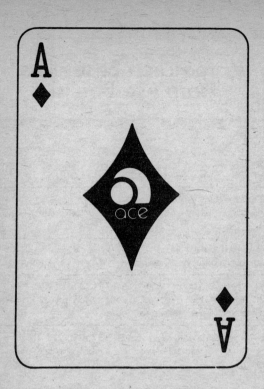

Don't Miss these Ace Romance Bestsellers!

74b

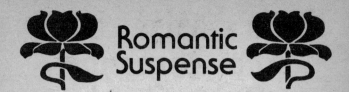